The Three Domains of Freedom

Each Moment is Yours
Your Life is Yours
Civilization is Yours

George Kinder

Acknowledgements:
Cover by Lydia Brown with George Kinder and Caspar David Friedrich. Special thanks to the Staatliche Museen zu Berlin.

Book Design by Lydia Brown
Illustrations by George Kinder and Lydia Brown
Photograph of author by Rachel Kinder

With tremendous gratitude to Kathy Lubar, Maryellen Grady, Lora Woodward, Lydia Brown, Joan Luzier, and Julian Powe.

ISBN: 978-1-960044-00-6

Copyright © George D. Kinder 2024

First Edition

All rights reserved. No part of this book may be reproduced or transmitted in any form or by any means, electronic or mechanical, including photocopying, recording, or by any information storage and retrieval system, without written permission from the author, except for the inclusion of brief quotations for review.

Printed in the United States of America

www.serenitypoint.org

Serenity Point Press

To all the Earth's creatures

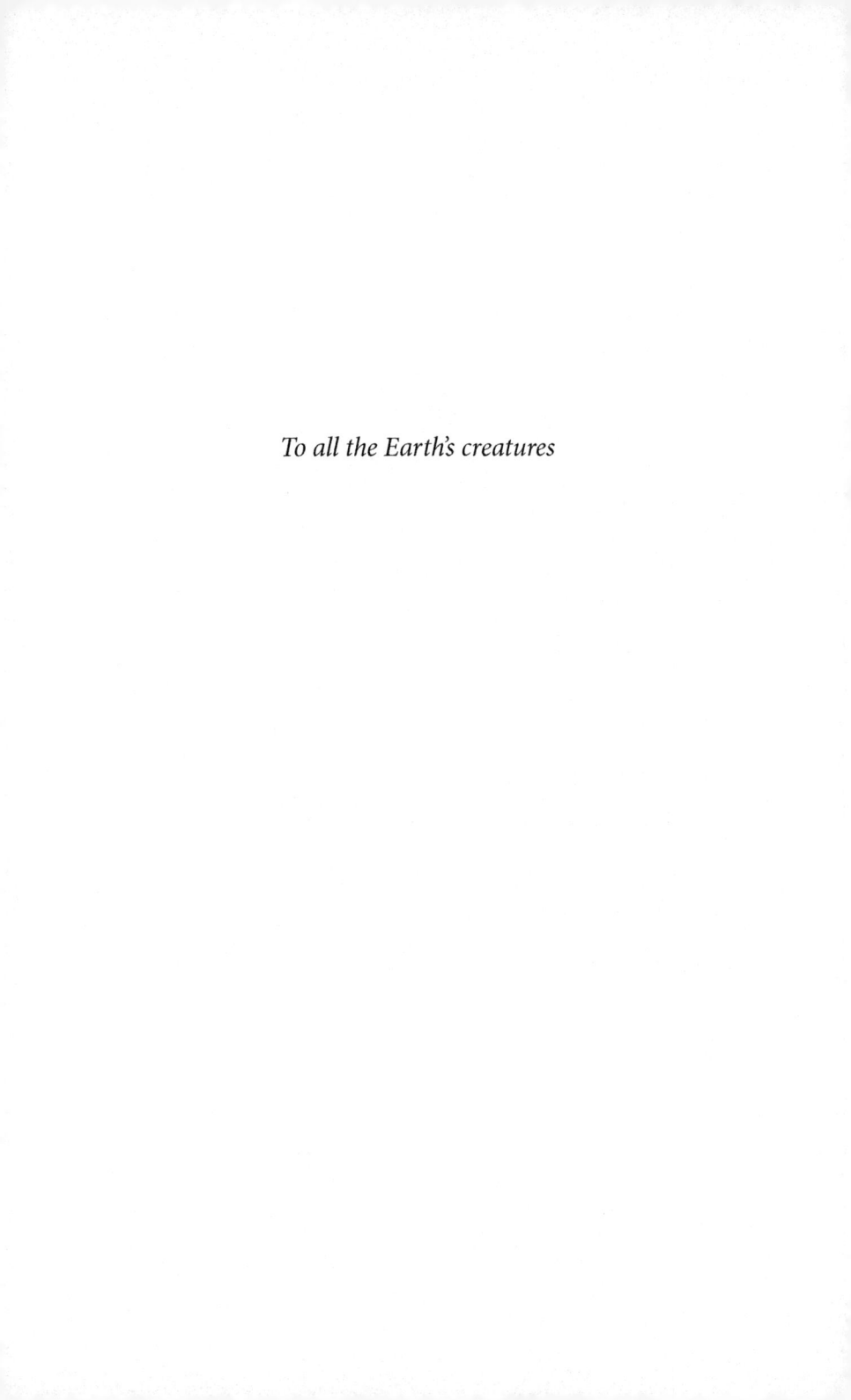

Table Of Contents

Foreword i

Introduction 1

Domain One: The Freedom of Moments.
  The Hidden Jewel 7

    Introduction 7

    The Practice 16

      The Map of Mindfulness 23

    What Could Possibly Get in the Way? 29

      Transforming Suffering into Wisdom 31

    What if We All Did It? 34

    Conclusion 36

Domain Two: The Freedom of Life.
  Your Birthright 39

    Introduction 39

    The Practice 45

      The Three Questions 45

      EVOKE® Life Planning Process 51

What Could Possibly Get in the Way?...................................59

What Happens If We All Do It?...64

Conclusion: Your Life is Yours. Putting the Freedom
of Moments into the Freedom of Your Life...................67

Domain Three: The Freedom of Civilization.
All Creatures Meant to Be Free...69

   Introduction..69

   The Practice..74

      Celebration..77

      Making it Happen.. 81

      Fiduciary In All Things (FIAT): It's Origins.................. 82

      Speaking Truth to Power,
      Bring Kindness to People... 93

      What Else Can We Do?
      What Other Action Can We Take?............................... 95

      What Could Possibly Get in the Way?........................... 98

      What if We All Did It?.. 109

   Conclusion to Civilization as our
   Third Domain of Freedom..112

Final Thoughts..115

Foreword

Through the summer of 2023, George Kinder would record a weekly meditation for my twenty-year-old daughter, Evie. Bedbound for 18 months, Evie was steadfastly recovering from long COVID, repairing and regenerating her nervous system. She described George's meditations as "melodic, warm, welcoming; a friend, a song."

Like many of us with the fortune to know George, Evie will have his song perched forever in her heart. This book gives many more of us the opportunity to absorb George's timely, inspiring song.

Energy pulsates through *The Three Domains of Freedom* as George illuminates his philosophy of consciousness, conscience, and connectedness. He calls us to celebration, action, and speaking truth to power. Essential wisdom for the twenty-first century.

George's song is of doing as much as daring. In our times of great peril and possibility, and with democracy still in its youth he urges us to action, inspiring us in short order to take humanity from adolescence to a sustainable, thriving adulthood.

Above all, George's song is one of being and of the elevation of the spirit. He ignites our imaginations to the highest and best aspects of ourselves (to honesty, truth, freedom, no war, humor, connectedness, integrity, beauty, equality of opportunity, compassion, courage, respect for nature, and morality) as George heard around the world in his conversations to envision a Golden Civilization. Here we encounter eternal truths and the cardinal virtues of wisdom, courage, temperance, and justice that run through all philosophical and religious traditions.

Two philosophers from the last three hundred and fifty years stand out for their strong resonance with George's stance in the twenty-first century - Baruch Spinoza (1632-1677) and John Rawls (1921-2002).

Spinoza was a passionate and outspoken defender of freedom, tolerance, and moderation, an early proponent of a democratic ideal and representative government. As his recent biographer Ian Buruma (*Spinoza: Freedom's Messiah*) writes, "Living now as we do at a time of book-banning, intellectual intolerance, religious bigotry and populist demagoguery, his radical advocacy of freedom still seems fresh and urgent."

Rawls produced *A Theory of Justice* in 1971 and *Political Liberalism* in 1993. He asked what "Justice" required of us. As in George's envisioning of a Golden Civilization, Rawls adopted "The Original Position," throwing our imagination forward to design a better society from the stance of not knowing what position in society we would then occupy (class, gender, ethnicity, income, sexuality, etc.). His resultant principles speak loudly to us in the 2020s: the principles of Liberty (the right for everyone to a range of basic freedoms that cannot be taken away from them); Economic Justice (equality of opportunity); Just Savings (all we do must be consistent with a basic commitment to social and environmental stewardship); and Duty of Civility (courtesy in debate and disagreement).

George Kinder is the John Rawls of the twenty-first century. His notions of freedom, fairness, equality of opportunity, dignity, stewardship, and justice pour forth from *The Three Domains of Freedom*. When Daniel Chandler speaks thus of John Rawls' presence and ideas in his recent book, *Free and Equal: What Would a Fair Society Look Like?* he could just as easily be speaking of George:

> *"We are at a cross roads with a strong need for moral ideas on justice, freedom, equality, backed up by practical ideas on how we can change our institutions – to build a better society – a kind of moral and political leadership that has been missing for years – to cut across social, cultural and political divisions to make a fundamentally moral argument about how and why we can change society for the better."*

Spinoza, Rawls, Kinder. Radical, moral voices calling us to freedom, to our higher, better selves. More than that, they are all much needed dishabituation entrepreneurs. Human beings habituate easily in service of survival and security; we respond less and less to things that are constant or change slowly. Dishabituation entrepreneurs alert us to what is dangerous before the temperature of the bath water becomes too much to bear. Through embrace of the Three Domains of Freedom, George urges us to wake up, to see clearly what threatens humanity and the planet, before it is too late.

> *"Now I'm awake to the world. I was asleep before. That's how we let it happen." (June Osborne/Offred, The Handmaid's Tale, Margaret Atwood)*

What George adds, and what differentiates his work from other contemporary political thinkers is that it goes from the personal to the social and back again - whereas other works operate at the social and systemic only.

As I think and act into my own continued embrace of the Three Domains of Freedom and my understanding of George's song, I see five motifs, echoing and recurring throughout, that I will hold especially dear:

> *Imagination and inspiration.* Humanity can choose to look at any arrangement and see not just what it is but also what it could be. George's song urges and supports us to liberate our creativity, to develop our individual and collective imagination to make essential breakthroughs.

> *Wonder and awe.* In our distracted times, the key in George's song is attention, "Prosoche" in the lexicon of the Stoics. With mindfulness, attend to the present moment, attend to the wonder within and around us, attend to each other, attend to our planet, attend to the future.

> *Breathe nature in.* Just as nature and the natural order are George's teachers, so do they become ours in the Three Domains of Freedom. As in his poetry, George teaches us to make nature part of us, to breathe it in. And here his song becomes a lament, expressing deep sorrow for humanity's violation of our relationship with nature, in both our inner and outer worlds.

Foreword

Appreciation of beauty. A poet himself, George's mind is full of his beloved Bach, Dante, Shakespeare, Blake, and the epic poets. George spends much time in the company of the masters who reach out to the archetypes and bring them into being for us in artistic form. They inspire him to his moral and spiritual vision.

Right habit, right way. Marcel Proust reminds us that, although habit may be how we give shape to our lives, it can also lull us into gliding across the surface of existence. We need to be dishabituation entrepreneurs, habitually! George offers us powerful habits across the Three Domains of Freedom that connect us to our higher selves.

George's song is of the ages, for freedom and for humanity. Above all, it is about dignity. In our era of extraordinary technological innovation, more and more civilization can strip away the dignity of human beings across the globe, layer by layer, often barbarically. George's refrain paints a path for restoring these layers of dignity, progressively and determinedly—for us, for our fellow human beings, for our civilization.

George's chorus rises at the end of each Domain of Freedom – "What If We All Did It?"

A chorus whistling us up. All of us, individually. All of us, collectively.

Indeed.

What if we all did it?

Julian Powe, London, April 2024

Introduction

Poor as a church mouse, my client on disability would come to my office for an hour each year to discuss his life and finances. There was a sureness about him that drew me in. His clarity of moments, of purpose in his life, and his engagement in the world inspired me.

Dedicated to the present moment, I'd often see him walking through Cambridge to the Zen Center. We'd exchange hearty hellos and pleasantries, and his celebration of life and of the lives around him was contagious. Despite significant physical and financial challenges, he remained deeply confident in himself. He embodied the essence of the Three Domains of Freedom. Each moment was precious to him, aware as he was of the fragility of life. His life purpose was central to him. And he engaged with civilization as if it was his to make, as if he was crafting it around him.

Each moment was his.

His life was his.

Civilization was his.

I am here to remind you that what was true for my client is also true for you and me: each moment is ours; our lives are ours; civilization is ours.

We can live in freedom.

◇◇◇◇◇◇◇◇◇◇◇

We live in a world of moments. Each arises fresh and unique. In any given hour, there are thousands of them, and in each of those moments, we can experience freedom.

Most of the time we race from task to task. And when we are not racing, we relentlessly scroll through our hand-held devices for news of the day, entertainment, or for our next task.

How often do you wish you were someplace else, doing something else?

How often in a day do you feel trapped, and yet continue to pursue the tasks at hand, not believing you can be free, not anticipating a moment of freedom until you get home from work, and even then, continuing to scroll through yet other relentless pursuits?

Not only have we lost the moments of our day, but the life we wanted to lead continually slips past. The vision of who we want to be feels beyond our grasp. We are trapped by our habits and by the paths civilization has made available to us, paths that only promise freedom many years away, hobbling into retirement. And even then, our moments are not ours, our lives are not ours, civilization is not ours.

My own experience of this was most poignant in the thirteen years I spent doing tax returns for a living, tied to an adding machine and a calculator, an office chair and a table, to volume after volume of the Internal Revenue Code, its cases and its regulations, to endless appointments and the relentless deadlines of the IRS. I felt cursed, stuck working in the world of money, tied to a clock, delivering nothing more than mere survival.

I couldn't find anyone to pay me to do what I loved, to write poetry or to meditate, but I recognized the privilege of working with all kinds of people and saw that I was bringing a kind of freedom to their lives.

After a few years of doing taxes for academics, therapists, and entrepreneurs around Cambridge, I saw that I could be more helpful (and make better money) if I took on all the financial issues for my clients, not just their taxes. So, I studied and became a financial planner.

Working to deliver comprehensive financial plans, I soon realized that my clients were no happier than I was, and that money was not the real issue for any of us. It wasn't the ticket to freedom. We wanted much that materialism had to offer, but we didn't want to do what seemed necessary to get it. Our passions were somewhere else. I came out of the 60s thinking everyone was "free, man," and we'd all live happy and joyous lives. But that wasn't what I was hearing from the thousand people that came through my practice. It wasn't what I was feeling either. It seemed we all felt as if our dreams were fading, as if we had begun to live in someone else's reality.

As I worked, I discovered there was a path to the freedom of moments, to freedom within each moment, and, as I learned financial planning, I discovered the path to the freedom of my life as well. Civilization may have failed me in its paths, I thought, but I was determined not to fail myself.

So, I began to craft a life where in every spare moment I lived the freedom I longed for – to practice meditation and to create art. I pursued money in my career, so I could have the time outside of work to pursue what I loved. Taxes would never be my passion. I was an artist, a lover of William Blake and Vincent Van Gogh. I wanted to live as a monk in the woods and experience moments one by one. I wanted a relationship and eventually a family. I was young, and I didn't understand how I could have all these things, given the economics of the world, but I was determined to make them possible. The irony was that it was there, as I was doing tax returns, that I discovered that each moment was mine and found the passion that would become my life plan.

How did I do it? I've been teaching what I have learned to people from all over the world for the past few decades. Now, I am ready to share my knowledge and practices with you in this book.

We are born to live in freedom. We feel it deep inside ourselves. We know it as a species. When you live your truth, nobody but you can ever be the boss of who you are.

And we are born to deliver freedom to others. My client, living his truth, delivered freedom to me in our brief encounters, though he might have thought it was the other way around. Inspired by him, as I've traveled the world, I've returned the favor a thousandfold. Whenever we take the

Introduction

time to listen to a person's dreams, we bring them the very freedom they describe. And freedom is contagious.

We have the power in our moments of freedom to call on infinite sources of energy and compassion to manifest both our own destiny and to help deliver our fellow human beings into their own destinies, each of them as vulnerable and as filled with promise as we ourselves have been.

Of all our freedoms, civilization may seem the most challenging to realize. Inequality and bigotry, corruption and violence, threats to democracy, the planet, and the truth concern us. Each of us feels subject to powers much greater than we are. As I developed the first and second domains of freedom within myself, I discovered the way to make civilization a domain of freedom as well. We are meant to experience civilization as a freedom, to create it for others and for generations to follow. I will share the way to live in freedom in civilization, even in the midst of our greatest challenges.

There are Three Domains of Freedom: each moment is yours; your life is yours; civilization is yours. Imagine if everyone you know lived with such freedom, everyone in the world. I hope to both inspire you and to provide a practical guide for accumulating the freedoms that will enrich your life and the lives of those around you. The world will be better for it.

Domain One: The Freedom of Moments

Domain One:

The Freedom of Moments. The Hidden Jewel.

Introduction

For the longest time I couldn't experience the present moment. I understood that we live in a world of moments, but they seemed mostly continuous. Surely what was important about them was their content not them in themselves. Then I learned mindfulness. Through mindfulness I realized that each moment, each one of them, is a hidden jewel, and in each of them you can be free.

Mindfulness is the practice of mastery of the present moment. It's a profound practice of experiencing reality directly, just as it is. As such it is relaxing yet energizing at the same time. Relaxing because it is authentic, in the natural flow of things, uninterrupted by thoughts. And energizing from the power of each moment to create the world anew. It's the mastery of the present moment that delivers all the mindfulness benefits that science describes and many more. A great mindfulness practice is about experiencing freedom

Domain One: The Freedom of Moments

in every moment. It is the practice that establishes and secures each moment as yours.

People used to think mindfulness was woo-woo. Now they are more likely to think it may be useful but time-consuming or boring. They suspect that if they could find their way through those two obstacles, they could improve their health and longevity, diminish their stress, and even accomplish greater success at work or at home or in sport. But mindfulness opens up another world. It reveals a jewel, hidden in each moment of our mundane existence, a jewel that cannot be accessed by microscope or telescope, not by computer nor by thought, but only directly. It can't be mediated.

It is an astonishing notion. Each moment is here for us, and in each of these we are meant to be free. It is even more astonishing when you realize that the only moment you've ever experienced in your whole life is the present moment. And yet it's never used up. It doesn't matter that you might have missed billions in your life already. It keeps arising, again and again!

Moreover, the present moment is the only moment where you experience freedom. You never experience it in the past or in the future. From the perspective of the First Domain of Freedom, our task is simple. To achieve the freedom of the present moment, we must wake up in each moment!

The structure of time and space, of the past and the future, is a history and a prophecy. It is like the outline of a dream that represents our material world. Science keeps analyzing the past and projecting the future as the only reality. Real they may be, but they pale in comparison to the reality of the present moment. If the present moment is the only moment we've ever experienced, a mastery of the present moment becomes a mastery of everything. With the practice that I will teach you, you will recognize how in any moment you can choose to be present and choose to be free.

◇◇◇◇◇◇◇◇◇◇◇◇

For over 50 years I've practiced meditation several hours a day. I've taught mindfulness for over 35 years in weekly classes and week-long retreats. I've written books about it. My life's work is the present moment.

How I got here was not always easy, but simple practices used daily keep the freedom of each moment fresh, accessible, and alive for me.

My early life included numerous solitary flashes of awakening, but I trudged the path that civilization provided, often not seeing beyond my daily tasks and obligations. Though periodically dramatic and exciting, it was also lonely and often a struggle. I'm probably not that different from other people in those regards, with the possible exception that I held a secret all-consuming passion for the growing number of remarkable experiences I could not explain.

Most of us have had profound, even spiritual, experiences in our lives, but we don't talk about them. Somehow, they make us feel special in a way that might seem arrogant or egocentric to others – or just strange. Even in a religious society, we can feel odd or shy to share. How much more in a secular society where there is little room for such revelations? They won't help you get a job or get married, have kids, or pay your bills.

What is the place of these experiences, I would wonder? What is their meaning? What should I do with them? Early on, I decided these profound moments were the most important things in my life and so, intermittent with my work and my relationships, and most often without anyone knowing, I pursued understanding them through my readings, through contemplative practices, and through nature. It was through them – by making them a priority in my life – that I found my way to the hidden jewel and the freedom it delivered, which I now find to be useful in every aspect of life.

It was hiding within me all along. There was nothing really to search for; freedom itself was there in every moment—unseen, but always there sustaining everything. It was particularly easy to experience it in nature. So, a great deal of my learning the mindfulness of moments was done outside, where moments change so quickly, and so beautifully, engaging each of our senses, touching us in different ways, and all the time.

When I look back at the successes in my life, the books, my relationships and family, my business, I attribute it all to my mindfulness practice. I'd thought I was searching for something, but mindfulness gave me the ability to experience freedom in each moment, to focus on anything that needed attention. It's given me sufficient ease to work with the problematic stuff, while giving me the energy, vitality, and confidence to accomplish much in each day. I owe everything to this practice.

The Hidden Jewel

Moments are the hidden jewels of life. Their value can't be calculated. Deluded by our mental maps of time and space to think of the present moment as merely a pivot in the continuity of time between the past and the future, we never recognize that the present moment is all we're given in life, all we ever experience, and perhaps all there is. But when we bring a sustained attention to the present moment, we soon realize that in every moment we have an opportunity to be free. The present moment reveals its magic and its riches. We discover that present moments are our fuel, our foundation, our sustenance, and our delight. Through mindfulness, they become both how we ground ourselves and our source of vitality, of explosive energy.

Imagine attending a family event and finding who you are in each moment, not defined by who someone expects you to be. Not defined by your aversions or by attachments or the tapestry of relationships, but just by the freshness of how you feel, how you experience each moment, your alertness, your love and compassion, your sense of comfort or discomfort, your experience of how the breeze comes through the screen, the colors and shapes of things around you, the smell of flowers and food, the kindness you feel in your heart, and, looking down, the minute sensations in every breath, all intermingled with momentary engagements with those you love or are troubled by, finding who you are, regardless of what comes up, even sadness, frustration, irritability. The world completely changes as we recognize that freedom is already here for us, all the time. Nobody can take it from us. Nobody.

Moments are a universal freedom available to everyone, the pulse of life itself. It may seem odd to say, but if you wish to experience the most extraordinary thing, experience impermanence, experience how moments arise and pass away. Don't think about them or analyze them, breaking them into past or future. Experience them now, again and again, as the present moment, in their arising and in their passing. This is the practice of mindfulness.

Gather a mastery of the present moment, and you will find freedom everywhere. It is abundant. The more you work with it, the better it becomes. By paying attention to your relationship to this moment, then this one and this one, you experience evolution inside yourself. The higher the quality of your attention the more you evolve and the more happiness you feel in your life. Evolution is not about becoming smarter. It's about becoming more awake.

The very first time you experience the present moment can be stunning. Or perhaps, like me, you have already experienced it intermittently in extraordinary moments throughout your life. One of my long-time meditation students shared with me that before she came to meditation, she had never experienced the present moment. When she finally did, it felt like freedom to her and at the same time it was a shock, as if she had done something wrong, as if she was in a forbidden place. It astonished her to discover that moments of freedom existed and that she had had access to them all along. She was stunned by how her mind, with all its complexity of thought, had brainwashed her to assume the hidden jewels of life could only be found in the past or in the future, in things she longed for or in stories or fantasies of herself, but never right here, right now.

As she accessed the present moment in her meditations, she began to understand how her mind had kept her trapped. She began to meditate every morning, looking to access the present moment and break open her day. She would meditate for as long as it took to feel the power of a single moment.

Her story reminds me of William Blake's famous quotation, encouraging us

> To see a World in a Grain of Sand
>
> And a Heaven in a Wild Flower,
>
> Hold Infinity in the palm of your hand,
>
> And Eternity in an hour.

Taking Blake's poem to heart, she has practiced meditation an hour a day for thirty years. Through her practice she learned to experience moments, and over time, she discovered for herself that the essence of freedom could be found in each one of them. Accessing the present moment helped her redirect her life path, to not get lost in her stories, and to see what's important.

You too can summon that freedom and the courage it takes to find it.

Each moment is yours.

When you experience the freedom of a moment you are completely here, rather than guided or trapped by the stories, the scenarios that play video loops in your mind. When you drop into just being here, there are three major experiences: you feel happiness, you feel clarity, you feel at ease. To be able to summon them at any moment is remarkable.

Domain One: The Freedom of Moments

In each moment you have access to these virtues. Mindfulness of moments brings them all: authenticity, comfort, peace, kindness, joy, tranquility, equanimity, vitality, generosity, delight, energy, patience, courage, and many more. You feel alive.

When I experience freedom, these virtues are available to me in every moment. There are so many moments where I used to be filled with chatter about myself, or with a mood that I'd latched onto. Now, I can walk through nature, walk to work, be engaged with my computer or with my children, do tasks around town and just be completely present, filled with delight, at ease, happy. You can choose to be in that place too.

What's wonderful is you can be in a setting where you don't feel these virtues, and you can cut right through it, bringing these qualities in. It impacts everything. Most important is what happens inside yourself; you're not trapped by what is going on around you. You experience being clear with no obstruction and no attachment. You see other people clearly and compassionately and can act with kindness. You see your thoughts and how they might obstruct you, but you let the problematic ones go and go to places that are helpful. You experience your feelings without getting stuck in them and instead, feel what's useful, informative, or profoundly human within them.

When you discover the secret of moments, you too can summon freedom from any place in time and in any circumstance. You have learned the mastery of the present moment.

As you let go of your self-stories to experience the moment, you cultivate selflessness, the virtue at the center of all virtues. Your relationships improve and you become a better listener. You don't feel the urge to react or cling to attachments.

How many times a day do you find yourself complaining about how your day is not yours? How you are not free?

Imagine if at each of those instances instead, you paused, stopped whatever was driving you from inside, and claimed that moment as yours. What would happen if your primary understanding as you went through your days was that each moment was yours? That every moment of your life was yours?

We have called the fruit of our practice, mastery of the present moment. Others have called it enlightenment or awakening or being reborn. I refer to it as authenticity or wisdom. What could be more authentic than to be right here right now?

So how do we accomplish this? What are the practices? How can we make the experience of the freedom of moments resilient and sustainable within us? What is the most efficient way for us to learn to access present moments, and how we can make each moment our own?

Let me share with you the practice.

The Practice

Now that you know the hidden jewels are there, what can you do so that in each moment you can access them?

The practice is very simple.[1] If you practice these steps for 20 to 30 minutes a day, it will make an enormous difference in your life. You will begin to recognize changes within a matter of weeks. You might already feel more ease or alertness in your life. You almost certainly will begin to experience that something has shifted, that something positive has begun to happen. The steadier and more long-term your practice becomes the more pronounced and recognizable the benefits will be.

For people who aren't doing mindfulness yet or don't know how to do it, I recommend starting with 30 minutes of formal practice each day. For those that practice mindfulness already, my recommendation would be to double your practice. You can't do too much. It becomes a strength that you can apply in many ways throughout your life.

Find a quiet place. Sit with your back relatively erect, your body stable and at ease. (This is often called a "sitting practice.") Make a commitment not to move, not even for

---

[1] See *Transforming Suffering into Wisdom: Mindfulness and The Art of Inner Listening,* George Kinder, Serenity Point Press, 2011, for a more in-depth survey of mindfulness practices. The book is a primer of dozens of mindfulness practices, both internal and external, meant to strengthen your meditation practice and to extend it into everyday life.
    Meditate with George Kinder: https://www.georgekinder.com/meditation

an itch. Of course, if you feel you might harm your body, it's important to shift your posture, moving as slowly and mindfully as you can. Every time you move you break your concentration and lose some depth. It may even feel as if you have to start your meditation over again.

You want to begin each practice by deepening your concentration. So close your eyes. Focus on the present moment, not your thoughts. We're used to thinking of thoughts as being the present moment, but we get lost in their storylines and their moods. Mindfulness starts as we let our thoughts go. Focus instead on feeling sensations inside your body, fleeting though they may be. The more fleeting they are the better. If they are clear enough for you to feel them, they are the expression of the present moment.

Ground yourself first by feeling the sensations in your body, and then, narrowing your focus, bring your attention to the sensations of breathing, either at the nostrils or at the belly. Follow these sensations, or return to them, experiencing them throughout the rest of your meditation as you let your thoughts go.

That's pretty much it. That's the essence of it, at least. It's very, very simple. Just bring your mind to these sensations, and every time your mind wanders, bring it back.

I find it useful to be aware of four categories of sensations:

- Temperature: Is the sensation cool or is it warm?
- Texture: Is it smooth or is it rough? Is it hard or is it soft? Is it tight or is it at ease?
- Quality of movement: Is it moving about or is it stationary?

- Dimensionality or shape: Does it feel like a point in space, a line, or something two- or three-dimensional?

For _each_ sensation, the question is how it *feels*, not how do you see it or what you think about it.

Simply be with the breath or return to the breath, feeling it each time you return. If you can't be with the breath, be with the present moment, whatever present moment is arising for you while you keep attempting to return to the breath.

If you can't somehow find either the present moment or the breath, notice *impermanence*, how things are changing, or how they have just changed. Notice how this moment is different from the moment that just passed. Label your experience 'impermanence.' The main practice is simply *returning*. In fact, the greatest value of the practice is in the returning, returning to the experience of the present moment, of sensations. It doesn't matter how long you have wandered or how difficult it is to stay. Just keep returning. Whether you primarily experience the breath, the present moment, or impermanence, your sustained practice of attention and of returning will bring you both exhilaration and peace.

It can be helpful and illuminating to notice, when your mind wanders, what pulls it away. Is it desire? Is it a fantasy? Is it aversion or lethargy? Is it a judgment or an opinion or planning? Is it a self-story? Is it grasping? Is it a mood or feeling? You will begin to see familiar patterns that make it easier to notice them when they arise and to let them go. But don't dwell on them, don't analyze them, or get lost in them. As soon as you've noticed, very simply, but directly, return to your breath. Over time, and beginning quite quickly, you will discover that being here, returning, brings more pleasure than wandering away.

As you practice, you're cultivating your quality of attention and your ability to focus. At first, you feel all thumbs, like learning to play the piano and you don't have a teacher. Keep at it and you begin to cultivate the present moment as if it were a new friendship or a garden you were planting. Maybe the next day your meditation won't be as good as the day before, but I guarantee that three weeks from now, the general quality of your attention is going to be better than it was in the first few days of your practice. Three weeks further on, your quality of attention is going to be even better, with more ease and more energy to boot.

Deepen your concentration by keeping the mind as single-pointed as you can, returning again and again to the sensations of the breath, and then, within that concentration and with mindfulness, begin to focus exclusively on the present moment and impermanence. As you move from concentration to mindfulness, you will find an open awareness that contacts moments, as if it were touching them.

You're cultivating a mastery of the present moment. It's a very simple thing. By doing this, you'll find that when you're with other people, or when you're engaging in any kind of activity, you will be more present. You've been practicing letting your self-thoughts go, letting your "I, me, mine" thoughts go, because that's the only way to be completely present with your sensations and in the moment. It's a practice of selflessness.

Part of the practice is not reacting to distractions. Make a commitment to not respond to pets or phones or people. Meditate in a place best suited for quiet. Set yourself up for success by preparing for possible distractions ahead of time. Let your family know that you're going to be busy for 30 minutes and they are not to disturb you unless it is an absolute emergency, close the door, turn your phone to silent. Give yourself permission to take this time for yourself. Those you live with may want you in the moment, but as they give you the space you need, they will value the person you become.

It's easy to get discouraged at the beginning. Make a time commitment to do it every day and keep to that time commitment no matter what. Make it a habit. It can be helpful to meditate in the same place and at the same time every day, so your body immediately feels relaxed when it goes there.

Over time you will find many variations to your practice. One of my favorite meditations came from practicing in nature. I call it my "sitting on the stoop" meditation. There is a ritual in Zen to ask the Master, "What is Enlightenment?" Countless responses have been made over centuries, most of them paradoxical or confusing at first. One of my favorite responses is, "When I'm sitting, I know that I'm sitting." "Sitting on the stoop" draws its wisdom from that response.

I spend much of my day in a writing and meditation cabin out a narrow hundred-yard peninsula from my home. The land juts into the center of a large pond. At the door of my cabin is a wooden platform barely large enough to fit two chairs. You will often find me sitting on one of them taking a break from the tasks of my day. At first you might have found me gazing at the pond just 10 yards away through a scrub of high blueberry bushes, moss, and maple leaves. But I soon learned it was more relaxing to just sit on the stoop, without gazing, without looking about. So that's what I do. I just sit on the stoop. I look down rather than look about, mostly at my torso and my knees and the boards and the ground shrub nearest me. Even when I hear a chipmunk or a bird moving through the bushes, rather than search for them, I just sit, feeling my body, the warmth of the sun or the coolness of the wind, feeling my breath, feeling the wonder of being in nature with its aromas and shifting sounds and shapes, just sitting on the stoop knowing that I am here, rather than chasing my thoughts or my attachments or aversions out into the world or into the past or the future.

I use a version of this meditation wherever I go, even when I'm driving or in a meeting or walking about or lying down. The frame I use for it is to ask myself the question, "How do I know that I am here?" Mostly I find the answer in my sensations and in my breathing, in my standing or sitting or walking about. I find what a wonderful thing it is just to be here.

It may seem astonishing, but the truth is, wherever you are you can practice. Not perhaps your 30 minutes a day, but often even in the most challenging situations there are pauses. In those pauses you can practice. Some pauses you can create yourself, just stopping mid-sentence and finding a few moments to notice how you are right here, right now. Be creative with it.

In the early days of meditating, of learning to make each moment yours, it is hard to believe that you can bring this practice of presence to every aspect of your life. You just think, "I'm putting in my dues. I'm going to practice my 30 minutes, and then I'm done for the day." But you are always breathing, twenty-four hours a day, and at some point, you realize that there are so many moments in your life you could bring the practice to. So, you begin to bring it into each of those moments, and it grows, whether it's by noticing the breath or feeling sensations in your body, or just becoming aware of the present moment, you are learning to claim each moment as your own, and to live in freedom all the time.

William Blake, in his illuminated epic poem *Milton* (35:42-45), reminds us of the power of accessing these moments:

> *There is a moment in each day that Satan cannot find*
>
> *Nor can his Watch Fiends find it, but the industrious find*
>
> *This moment and it multiply, and when it once is found*
>
> *It renovates every moment of the day if rightly placed.*

This has certainly been true for me. Since early 2020, I've suffered from the fatigue of long-haul COVID. As a consequence, I upped my mindfulness practice. Rather than being glum and thinking "I can't do this," or "I can't do that" and despite my fatigue, I live in an action-oriented world, as I meet each moment of experience.

Mindfulness practice is something that you can do all your life and in almost any condition. You may not notice it at first, and sometimes it may even feel as if the opposite is true, but mindfulness strengthens each time you practice it. Your focus becomes stronger, your stress lessens, you heal more quickly. But most of all from doing the practice, you experience greater freedom throughout your life, greater happiness, and greater resilience, a greater readiness to be present with whatever life brings. It's no wonder that's the case, as the practice itself is to just be here, to be present, alert in each moment.

Despite the symptoms of long COVID, I've been surprisingly productive. I credit my meditation practice for providing a wellspring of energy and presence during this period. In fact, if I don't feel free, if I begin to shut down, I drop what I'm doing and practice the presence of moments, then and there.

The Map of Mindfulness

There is a logic to how mindfulness works, almost a science to it. As I was writing *A Golden Civilization & The Map of Mindfulness*, I was stunned to realize how the present moment, which is the only moment we have ever experienced, is absent from our maps of time and space. So, I created a map of mindfulness and of the present moment to show how they work, to clarify how the universe works, what the relationship with time and space to the present moment is, and what that relationship says about our place in the universe.

Domain One: The Freedom of Moments

The Map of Mindfulness
Listening to the Origins of Things

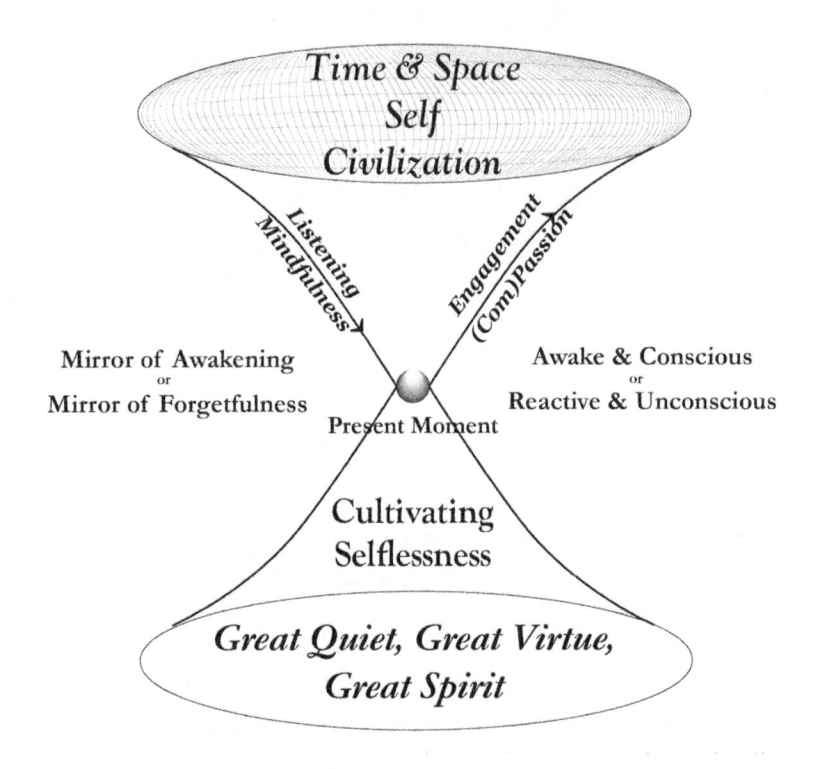

Time & Space
Self
Civilization

Listening
Mindfulness

Engagement
(Com)Passion

Mirror of Awakening
or
Mirror of Forgetfulness

Awake & Conscious
or
Reactive & Unconscious

Present Moment

Cultivating
Selflessness

Great Quiet, Great Virtue,
Great Spirit

From *A Golden Civilization & The Map of Mindfulness*

"Eternity is in love with the productions of time"

William Blake

Figure 1. The Map of Mindfulness

This image shows the relationship between time and space and the present moment and what humans have the potential to access when bringing their attention to the present moment.

The Map of Mindfulness can be difficult to understand at first.[2] We are tied to the past and future in complex and deeply rooted ways. Our usual map of time and space is seen in the image as an oval above the present moment. We fill it with artifacts and with projections of the past and the future, with self-stories, strategies of acquisition, and all the products of civilization. Broken into boxes and cells, it is confining, useful for analytics but not true to our experience. Rather, it is like a mirage of an oasis in the desert that fills our mind with distractions from the present moment.

The map shows the present moment and our relationship to it at the center of the map, just as it is at the center of our experience. It is fundamental rather than a mere artifact of space and time. Present moments are the real thing, each of them more real than the relics of time and space that they contain. Your authenticity and freedom in each moment is more real than your story. Each moment, directly experienced, returns us to who we are, to what it is to be right here.

In the Map of Mindfulness, you can see the realm of great peace we experience in meditation, a realm of virtue, as real, as palpable, as natural as our experience of time and space. It is accessed by our concentration on and by our returning to the present moment. We can discover it as a transcendent moment, a spiritual experience, an experience of vastness or kindness, and, when necessary, as a moment of courage.

The Map of Mindfulness gives us a way of understanding the world that's more accurate, more tuned into who we

---

2   See *A Golden Civilization & The Map of Mindfulness*, George Kinder, Serenity Point Press, 2018, for more detailed descriptions of the map. Also, at www.georgekinder.com you can find a video description.

are, than our traditional maps of time and space, where the present moment is ephemeral, and virtues are relegated to religion and philosophy rather than understood as part of the fundamental fabric of life.

The Map of Mindfulness is more accurate because it includes us. The quality of our attention, our relationship to the present moment, determines whether we experience freedom in life or feel trapped and imprisoned, reactive, and forgetful instead. This is why a practice toward the mastery of the present moment is so valuable. It is a mastery of the universe as it is.

On the map, you can see how mindfulness fills the world with selflessness. When, in meditation, we meet the present moment, there's no thought about one's self, neither in the past nor in the future. There's just the experience of air in the nostrils, of the belly moving up and down or in and out.

We have a choice, to meet each moment directly and in full consciousness or to react, unconscious and forgetful. When we see the present moment directly, we have simultaneous access to the world as we have come to know it, and to the world of virtue, spirit, and peace.

Consciousness is often thought of as either residing exclusively in the top oval, the cartesian domain of science, space-time, and evolutionary biology, or it is thought of as exclusively residing in the bottom oval of great peace, virtue, and spirit. It is approached either as something that evolved over time, coming to fruition in the human brain, something that can be analyzed, dissected, and identified in its mechanical place in the world like any other scientific object. Or it is understood as "the whole thing" almost as if it were God, encompassing everything, underlying everything.

But what if consciousness is neither of these things? What if it is always, and only tied to the moment in which it arises? After all that is how we experience it. And what if there is always a quality or degree to that consciousness ranging from clear and awake, to unclear, asleep, and unconscious? And our task is to wake up, to directly see the nature of things, in each moment to become free, and to use our innovation and creativity, of acting in equal measures passionate and compassionate, to wake the world up.

That within each experience of the present moment is the opportunity to wake up changes everything. Where we used to experience impermanence from the standpoint of aging and loss, as creatures on the grid of time and space, we can now see it in moments, as the onrushing opportunity to be free. Arising out of space and time it keeps opening hidden jewels of freedom to us in the guise of the present moment.

One of the great things about teaching mindfulness for the past 35 years is that I have been able to watch people who have strong daily practices deepen in other ways as a consequence. I've seen many examples of people letting go and finding more and more happiness in their lives. I've seen people become more and more virtuous, more compassionate, and kind.

You might wonder, does our experience of freedom and happiness from mastery of the present moment make any difference in the world? Certainly, these experiences make a difference in our own lives, but now, studies are showing that happiness and other virtues are contagious. They spread

Domain One: The Freedom of Moments

across the tapestry of time and space, from creature to creature. When we discover our authenticity through the mastery of the present moment, we bring its freedom into the world around us, moments of freedom that transform everything.

Each moment is extraordinary, unique, a gem, and each of them disappears never to be seen again. None of them has a self, not even an identity like a rock or a teacup or a tweet. But as they pass, each of them is yours. And in each of those moments you can be free.

What Could Possibly Get in the Way of our Achieving the Freedom of Moments?

The first minutes of meditation are often unsatisfactory as we are still lost in our stories, or in the daily news. It is difficult to find the breath when we are compelled by responsibilities or tasks, hear the ping of a text message or an email, or see the lunch on the counter our child forgot to take to school. It is not unusual in those first minutes to feel like jumping out of our skin! Or to say to yourself, "I can't meditate today."

What I have learned over the years, is that a "bad" meditation is a good meditation, perhaps even the best of meditations. It is in those moments, as agitated as they seem, that we are at our cutting edge of awareness and of awakening. It is those moments that each of us is meant to transform and to claim as our own. And in time, we will, if we maintain our practice of returning, as difficult as it feels, rather than running away.

I now find these challenges to my meditation to be the most beautiful thing, rather than an obstacle. As we ask what could possibly get in the way, we can feel our habits and "to do's" right where we most long for the experience of the present moment and its depths of peace. Now, I think of the Japanese aesthetic of *wabi-sabi*, where the beautiful is intentionally broken by imperfection, much as the wholeness of any experience is broken by impermanence.

As Leonard Cohen says, "That's how the light gets in." The secret is to keep practicing.

The biggest barrier to your success in claiming each moment as yours is going to be you, you and your grasping nature wrapping itself around your jobs, your family, your responsibilities. The past and the future get in the way. Whenever you start telling yourself a story about the future, where are you? You've lost the present moment. And when you wander back to the past, whether to feel guilt or to celebrate, watch out! You're getting attached. You're not there in the present moment either. What's amazing is that the simple practice of returning to the present moment cuts through these barriers.

Some of the classic obstacles to attaining freedom of moments are attachment, desire, aversion, restlessness, lethargy, and doubt. Each gets in the way of a "good" meditation or of forming a meditation habit. We can experience each of these obstacles as an energy or a mood or a story, often about ourselves. It is us getting in our own way. It is easy to say, "let go of your attachments." Many teachers will tell you that is the secret to freedom, but it is very difficult to do. If you find it difficult you might try instead to meditate only on moments that are already free, not sticky with attachment. Notice only them as you practice and throughout your day.

I've learned to meditate only on objects I can't get attached to, I can't cling to, I can't hold onto. Gradually that freedom spreads to everything in your life. Choose mindfulness objects that are clear and precise, but neutral, even boring, and that pass away before you can grasp them.

Practice with meditation objects that are already free. The breath, a breeze, a footfall, any sensation that passes as quickly as it arises and that is impossible to call back. Momentary sensations, impermanent sensations, these are already free.

Make impermanence your friend. It's the boring or the incidental moments that are the key. They are hidden jewels, like the present moment, because they are ungrasped and ungraspable. They are already free.

You lose the present moment every time you become attached. Stay with experiences that you can't get attached to, whether walking, standing, sitting, or lying down. Throughout your days, cultivate this mastery of freedom in the present moment.

Both the practicalities and the noisy humdrum of life can feel like obstacles. Choosing a quiet place to practice at the same time every day will help you. It's also helpful to surround yourself with people who are respectful of your practice. Consider finding a teacher, joining a group, or using a meditation app.

Transforming Suffering into Wisdom

It's particularly hard for us to practice when genuine tragedy strikes or strikes the world around us. And yet how valuable in each of those places it is to find moments of peace and clarity and to model it for others.

There are many moments in each day where I experience freedom and its delight. And there are extraordinary times of practice where I cultivate the present moment for hours in everything I do. But there are also moments where I suffer or am distracted. Each time I have learned those difficult moments were there for a reason. They were there to wake me up, to expand my freedom to another place, in yet another direction. And each time I find my way here. Right here. It's the evolution of awakening. Each day we learn, grow, change, and adapt, in order to experience greater and greater levels of freedom, of authenticity, of love, of who we really are.

A major theme in my book of meditation practices, *Transforming Suffering into Wisdom*, is how difficult emotions get hooked to stories about ourselves. That's how they create suffering. When we watch moments arising and passing away, what we discover is that suffering is always composed of structures of attachment, of thoughts hooked to feelings. I call them "structures of suffering." Through practice, I learned that if I *let my thoughts go and let my feelings be*, meeting each of my feelings as if it were a set of momentary sensations in the body, then quite quickly I could find my way back to the present moment. There, more than anywhere, it seemed, right in the midst of these difficult feelings, I found the hidden jewel. Even now, each time it happens it feels extraordinary. Just by coming back to the actual moment of experience, however dark it feels, we transform our suffering into wisdom.

One of my students for many weeks was plagued with unstoppable anxiety that sapped her self-worth, left her sleepless night after night, and filled her days and her daily activities with dread. But within just a few days of doing

The Hidden Jewel

this practice, of constantly and with great determination following this formula, she discovered her anxiety first as mere sensations, and then miraculously it was gone, as if it had never been there, replaced with lightness and joy. From that point on and throughout her life, whenever she felt anxious, she found herself quickly able to let the *thoughts* go that were tied to her anxiety and feel instead the *sensations* of anxiety in her body. They brought her to the present moment, often filled with feeling, but humane and no longer trapped in dread.

You will find the greatest resource you have is the steadiness of your practice. Commit yourself to it. Remind yourself every day, you're going to do this. In any moment you can find the Freedom of Moments – not just in formal meditation practice. You just come back to your body. Wherever you go you can sit on your stoop. It doesn't matter where you are, you can always ask yourself, "How do I know I am here?" You will always have moments. Each moment is yours.

What if We All Did It?

Imagine if all of us achieved the mastery of moments, if each of us could feel at any moment, the comfort and presence of just being here. We would feel it in each person we met. As if the world itself were authentic, trustworthy, and free.

The primary resource in our lives, aside from ourselves, is time, moments of time. Each moment can be a land of freedom for us, a source of energy and opportunity and wisdom. The future may be in short supply, after all you can never really experience it, but the present moment is abundant. Imagine the impact – eight billion moments of freedom from eight billion people, all realized together in a fraction of a second and delivered again and again – moment after moment flourishing into the world.

Even the hierarchies of power that place their own interests (and the interests of those who control them or own them) above those of the communities they engage with, above the planet and even above democracy, can't stand in our way. How can they touch the freedom of moments when it is recognized and has been made accessible to each one of us?

If all of us practiced this mastery of moments, civilization would be transformed. There would be a degree of peace and kindness in the world that the world has never seen. There would be energy and vitality, a sense of authenticity and trust amongst us all. There would be wisdom in everyone we met.

The Hidden Jewel

◇◇◇◇◇◇◇◇◇◇◇

The notion that each moment is yours is liberating. Millions of moments a day are yours. Totally yours. How many of them do you claim? Just think how efficient we could be with our lives. (I was once trained as an economist after all!) Mastery of moments means that I can renew myself all the time, make myself better, more open, more generous, more energetic, more authentic, just by coming back to the practice of moments. It is joyous to know that I'm not stuck in life, not at any time. I can always return to being here and know that the work I'm doing to be here is a work that delivers freedom wherever I go.

If all of us were to claim the First Domain of Freedom, were to understand that indeed each moment is ours, our map of spacetime and the world would shift from cartesian maps to Maps of Mindfulness. The map makes clear that every single moment has purpose in civilization as we make each moment ours. The world itself becomes virtuous, peaceful, awake, simply through our mastery of the present moment.

Conclusion

The First Domain of Freedom is the deepest and most fundamental. Nothing is more powerful than the present moment. No force in the universe can stop it from arising or prevent it from disappearing.

But what is most stunning about the moment, is its humanity. Mindfulness of moments clears away everything inhumane, so that the present moment may nourish our humanity, making it our home.

We were born to be free, the first domain proclaims it, and the Map of Mindfulness shows us how. All we need to do is pay attention to what the universe is – explosions of present moments and our engagements with them, our relationships to them. Simply by paying attention, our arrogance and self-centeredness diminish. Our humanity flourishes. We become what our name suggests, creatures of wisdom, *Homo sapiens*. This is what it means to be free. To be ourselves.

What does this say about the universe? It is creaturely and humane, not a machine nor a physics. The practice of mindfulness reveals the humanity within it. Our ecosystems and our planet require that depth of humanity from us to function at their best.

Until we realize that each moment is ours and that it is a domain of freedom, we misread everything about our world. Even in our science we misread time and space. They become realms of acquisition powered by greed and fear.

The Hidden Jewel

The First Domain of Freedom gives us the ability to be here even in the most difficult of times and with the most difficult feelings in a way that transforms our suffering into wisdom. With our practice of moments, we wake up rather than react, discovering how to be more of who we are.

Look down for a moment, as if you were sitting on your stoop. Feel your presence. Relax, find your breath, pause. Feel being right here. You'll find that listening to yourself in this way, without stories, you become a far better listener to others and to the whole world around you.

So, which world do you live in?

Do you live in a world filled with tasks and responsibilities – where too often you find yourself complaining that your moments are not yours, where too seldom you feel free?

Or do you live in a world of moments where each one of them is yours and spread through those moments is a tapestry of tasks and projects of your own choice.

Each moment is yours.

This moment is yours.

It is a domain of freedom.

Domain Two: The Freedom of Life

Domain Two:

The Freedom of Life. Your Birthright.

You will know your vocation by the joy that it brings you. You will know. You will know when it's right.
— **Dorothy Day**

A sense of calm came over me. More and more often I found myself thinking, "This is where I belong. This is what I came into this world to do."
— *Jane Goodall*

Introduction

For most of us, the Second Domain of Freedom is the most important of the three domains because it's "who we are." It's how we think of ourselves, or how we want to think of ourselves. It's our life. It's what we are most passionate about, what gives our life purpose and authenticity. It's something each of us can claim.

Moments may seem hard to find, or abstract compared to this, and civilization may feel too daunting. But delivering the life that most inspires us is something we can put all of our energy into when we see how possible it is. That's what the Second Domain of Freedom delivers. And as we accomplish our inspiring life, we gain confidence and ease in the First and Third Domains of Freedom as well. In fact, often they are both already part of our vision of an inspiring life.

When considering what is possible for us, we often think of money as our primary obstacle. And certainly, a proper relationship with money establishes and secures our life as ours, whether we are rich or poor. Note, I didn't say a proper amount. It is not so much the amount of money as our relationship to it and how we use it that sets us free. Too many people use money to fill holes of longing in their lives, rather than for the purpose of delivering themselves into their lives of freedom. If they were clear what that dream of freedom was and how they could deliver it, they would passionately make it happen starting right now. Money would not stand in their way. It would help to set them free.

Some people naturally live in a state of freedom, living the life they were meant to live. How inspiring! But if you are not one of those people, there is a great methodology called "life planning" that ensures you live it, that puts your dreams first and then provides the path to live into them. I know all about it because I designed it from my own struggles and have since taught it to thousands of people from over thirty countries for the past thirty years.

Even when I did tax returns for a living, I was determined to be free. I was passionate about it. Not only is each moment yours, but your life is yours. It's the story you are meant to live.

The vision we have for our life is profound and powerful. Conscious or not, we live by it. To claim it as a vision of freedom, is worth letting go of all our excuses.

Your life is yours.

It's a domain of freedom.

◇◇◇◇◇◇◇◇◇◇◇◇

In the Second Domain of Freedom, our life itself becomes a Path of Awakening for us, our vehicle to freedom.

Are you living your life of freedom? Are you calling the shots, or do you feel like someone else is pulling the strings? Parents, corporations, the government, bosses, spouses, your community, your kids, even money all vie for you to follow their set of rules. It's easy to get confused and lose your sense of self. I've been there. In early adulthood I had to fight to live in freedom.

Now I fill my life with what I love to do, and what I once experienced as "chores" or "responsibilities" I now see as part of that love, part of my path to freedom.

For the 13 years I was doing tax returns for a living, I was conflicted. I longed to live in freedom. But even when I was doing the tax returns themselves, lost in long evening or weekend hours, at my lowest or most stressful points, I would pause and remind myself of its purpose. I was doing this work to deliver myself into freedom. And I would then and there find my joy as if I were already living that freedom. I would suddenly see things I loved about the job, its perfections of clarity and truth, its compassionate purpose for my clients, its mastery of complex situations, and I would share my joy just by my attitude of freedom with those around me.

After a long day's work, I would walk 20 minutes home. The walks were a favorite part of my day. I loved being in the weather, in the moment, dropping all my attachments. I loved learning how to be at ease at the end of a jam-packed day. Each walk was meaningful, and when I got home, I would drop my backpack on the table and race out the back door to my porch, just big enough for the door to open, and I would sit on a chair to read books and poetry, to be in nature, and to meditate, in all kinds of weather. Even then I loved sitting on a stoop!

In winter, I would pile blankets on top of the coat I was already wearing. In the summer, when the generator from the store next door would blare, obscuring the songs of birds, I would remind myself, "Hey, man, these are your moments of freedom. Your freedom will only grow from here. You're doing this so you can *live* in nature, so you can write and meditate. You're doing this so you can be free. You live simply, saving money so that you can be free." And I did. I didn't have a car. I lived in a small apartment, and I chose that life for many years because of what it would afford me later.

Your life is yours.

Each of us is meant to craft our own life. If you want to be free, if you want to live your life with freedom, you can do it. You are meant to create your dream of freedom and to deliver it into the world. It is your birthright. It is your responsibility to yourself and to the world.

Your Birthright

In the struggles of those early years, I began to craft the methodology I now call life planning to help me claim my life as mine. After reading about the Second Domain of Freedom, you'll understand the rudiments of life planning and you will claim what matters most to you as well.

For most of us, there is something that's not quite accomplished, not quite delivered, some passionate pursuit remains on the table. We say, "I'll get to that," and life moves on. It is not unusual that we don't ever get to it. In life planning that doesn't happen. It's time to take your life back. It's your life. You too can live in freedom.

I've seen thousands of life plans over the years. I've seen people wake up to the fact that because of money and the expectations they feel from others they've driven themselves into a life where they're working 60-70 hours a week and more. They're eaten away at, not having the relationship with their kids or their spouse that they want. They're not nearly as productive as they might be, and they're certainly not fulfilled. There is no flourishing available for them to deliver themselves with authenticity or vitality to the people around them.

Life planning is a process that helps you identify what would bring the greatest fulfillment for you. Where you are off-balance, it identifies quickly how to gain the clarity, confidence, and gumption to re-negotiate your life. You'll know exactly what you're negotiating for, whether it's to be present for your family or to write that book that's been in the back of your mind for years. You'll find that you are far more vital and happier in every aspect of your life when you live your life plan. Everybody benefits when you are living into your life plan, your family, your friends and co-workers, all the people around you.

Everyone I know who's been life planned feels that their life is theirs, that they are creating it. They are bursting with freedom and bringing it to everybody they know.

The Practice

The Three Questions

The thousand clients I worked with over the years had something in common: They weren't living the lives they wanted.

Most of us deny our ability to live the lives we most desire because we think we need more resources, more money. Then we dive into the money world and forget what the lives we desired were going to be. Instead of delivering those lives to ourselves, we begin to measure our freedom by incrementally increasing amounts of money, whether earned or saved.

Thinking myself that money was the problem, I studied financial planning and became a CERTIFIED FINANCIAL PLANNER™ practitioner, hoping to find a way free. What I discovered surprised me. As valuable as learning financial skills was for me, far more important was my passion for freedom. That passion, even then, was delivering freedom into my life every day. Perhaps, I thought, if I could help my clients identify their own passions, I could help them live with more vitality the lives they most wanted to live.

So as a financial planner, I created exercises to understand what each of us longs for, what might deliver a similar passion to everyone who did them. I did them myself, and then shared them with my clients. Though I train the use of several approaches, the Three Questions, both playful and profound, stand out. Linked together they help shift our preoccupation with money to what is more meaningful, to legacy, passion, and purpose. They have become a powerful technique used by financial planners and coaches all over the world to help their clients cut through the web that society and money weave, so they can see their passionate purpose with clarity and act on it.

If you'd like to do them with me, get a piece of paper and pen to write down your responses to the following prompts.

> *The first question asks you to imagine you have all the money that you need for the rest of your life. What would you do? How would you spend your time? How would you live?*
>
> *Go on, dream!*

Your Birthright

The first question is like a warm-up for the next two. It gets you thinking about the many ways your life could be improved, ways you could have more freedom and more fun. It's like winning the lottery or being a kid going to Disneyland, finally! You get whatever you want. All your needs are taken care of. Though you may not achieve everything you've listed in your life, a great many of them are within reach.

The second question goes deeper. It's meant to be reflective. It moves us to the vulnerability of being human, to our fragility, which still has its anticipations.

> *Imagine that you go to the doctor and the doctor says, "I'm terribly sorry. You have a rare ailment, and you only have five to 10 years left to live. You'll be healthy during the time you're alive, but, sometime between the fifth year and the tenth year, you're just going to keel over. You don't know when that moment will be." You get five good years, maybe 10, that's it. What would you do with your life?*

Domain Two: The Freedom of Life

The second question addresses what is more important to you than money: your life and your time. Money can't do anything to help you here. You've just got these five to 10 years. The question broaches your legacy and purpose, the meaning of your life, with its reflection on death. Often, relationships come to the foreground more than they did in the first question, although there are frequent surprises.

The third question goes to the heart of legacy and gets to the essence of what it means to have a life, your life, right now. Your life is yours, not anybody else's. It's a domain of freedom. How do you make it yours?

> *This time the doctor has much worse news for you. You've got 24 hours left. That's it. The question is not what you would do with the time remaining. The question is, reflecting on your life in this moment and thinking about all the things that you have anticipated doing, what did you miss? Who did you not get to be? What did you not get to do?*

More than Question One or Question Two, this is truly a legacy question. Often the answers to Question Three, even when they seem impossible, form a foundation for the best life we could possibly live, the one not yet fully crafted, the one we put all our passion into. This is where we begin to take ownership of our life, reflecting on "Who did I not get to be?" and, with 24 hours left, "What do I regret not doing?"

Pour yourself into your answers. Then, once you have written them down, reframe your responses and imagine how you might now deliver each of them into the world. Where something seems impossible, imagine coming so close to accomplishing it, or something like it, and filling in the picture with so much life that there is no longer regret, but rather joy, aspiration, and a fullness of heart.

Often responses to the third question involve family or your creativity or living your values more deeply. Outwardly, it can involve giving back to the community or to the planet, or designing the ideal environment where you might live. It doesn't require winning the lottery. Money is not the primary constraint. It's time. And the truth is, right now most of us have the time to accomplish many of these things. It may require finding a few more hours a day to make them happen. But if it amounted to just a few hours a day or a day a week, couldn't you figure that out to live your life of freedom? People get very creative when they are energized to make a more ideal life happen.

When you claim your life and go for it, you gain great vitality. If suddenly you felt 20% more energized, imagine how much more you could accomplish in your life. It's time you gave that to yourself. And to your family, and to the world.

Domain Two: The Freedom of Life

When life planning clients, I craft a vision of their new life as they've described it in their answers to the Three Questions. I call it "lighting the torch." I paint a picture of them actualizing (or vigorously on their way to actualizing) every element of their third question within a period of months. Never more than two or three years. I include many elements from their second question and sprinkle in some from their first question as well.

The purpose of the vision is for clients to feel the sudden burst of freedom that comes from the experience of living the life of their dreams. Experiencing it even for a moment makes it more likely to occur, and if the torch is spot on, no one can refuse it. I then ask them to spend the next week or two living into the dream, imagining making it happen.

Your life is yours. The Three Questions is a tool for understanding what makes you uniquely you. It offers insight into who you're meant to be. And if you listen, its inspiration will give you the energy and imagination to make it happen.

Every single person that I've guided through the Three Questions found something important that they had not yet delivered on. How can that be? We live in one of the richest and freest cultures the world has ever seen, yet every single person that came in to work with me had something that they weren't delivering to themselves. Because of life planning people all over the world now live a life that is passionately theirs, complete, without leaving anything out.

I challenge you to live so that when you die, you can say, "I know I've done it. I have no regrets. I've lived the life I was meant to live."

EVOKE® Life Planning Process

The Three Questions are a tool from the EVOKE Life Planning process, which thousands of financial life planners from many countries use with their clients. I created the methodology a few years after publishing my first book on money, *The Seven Stages of Money Maturity*.[3] I was leading workshops based on the teachings in the book at financial advice conferences where advisors were internalizing the stages as a psychology or philosophy of money. They listened better to their clients and showed more interest in them, but they weren't quite getting the results I was having. I came to realize that what these advisors really needed was a replicable method to guide their clients into their dreams of freedom. EVOKE is that process, a model for delivering someone into their life plan.

EVOKE is an acronym that stands for the five phases in a life planning engagement: Exploration, Vision, Obstacles, Knowledge, and Execution. You can go through the process on your own,[4] or you can find a professional that's been trained to guide you through the process.[5]

---

3   *The Seven Stages of Money Maturity:* Understanding the Spirit and Value of Money in Your Life. George Kinder, Dell, 1999. *The Seven Stages* launched the Life Planning movement.
4   The website *lifeplanningforyou.com*, created by Kinder Institute of Life Planning, offers a free do-it-yourself experience for anyone to access the life planning process. The website accompanies George Kinder's book, *Life Planning for You: How to Design & Deliver the Life of Your Dreams*, Serenity Point Press, 2014.
5   Find Registered Life Planner® professionals all over the world at the Kinder Institute of Life Planning's "Find a Life Planner" search: *kinderinstitute.com/planner-search/*.

Simply put, the first step is to listen to yourself, to what's important to you, to who you really are (Exploration). Next, you craft a vision of how you want to be in the world, of who you want to be (Vision). Then, you look at the obstacles to that vision and, inspired by your vision, you come up with creative and actionable steps to overcome them (Obstacles). Fourth, you gather resources and put a plan in place (Knowledge). Last, you implement the plan (Execution). It's a simple but effective method for creating a hero's journey of your life. In *Life Planning for You*, and its accompanying free, do-it-yourself website, you will find more detail along with a step-by-step process.

One of the Vision exercises I love that supports the Three Questions in designing "the torch" is called Ideal Day, Ideal Week, Ideal Year. In it you imagine you are completely free to live your life as you like. Imagine a typical day from the moment you wake up till the moment you go to sleep and write down exactly how you would spend it, hour by hour, if you were free to design it just as you would like. Now design your ideal week which might have variations to the weekdays and weekend. Write down in detail how you want to spend your days. Then do your Ideal Year, going month to month. Where would you want to be in July? Or September? What would you be doing? It's fun to do this exercise and can be both liberating and clarifying for you as you claim your life as yours.

Of the many amazing things that come out of EVOKE, there are five categories that people come to again and again in their torches. I call them the five pursuits:

- Relationships and family
- Spirit or values

- Creativity—traditional arts or business, entrepreneurship
- Giving back to the community
- Environment or nature

I've seen thousands of clients come alive through these engagements and begin living on all their cylinders.

A dear friend in the UK was just beginning his family, and he wanted to take them to Lapland to see the reindeer and make a lasting memory for the whole family. It was a thrill to see him count the days till he could give that gift to his children and experience it as a father. Whenever I talked with him, he would tell me the number of days left.

Your life is yours. You design it. You deliver it.

Life plans are dynamic. When you revisit your plan, you can create something new each time. You could decide that what you've described is still what you're aiming for, or you might pivot completely.

It's worth reviewing your vision and the responses to your Three Questions and the Ideal Day, Ideal Week, and Ideal Year exercises regularly, even if just to relive the experience. Set a meeting with yourself once a quarter or once a year to revisit them or do so randomly or when you're feeling down. Ask yourself, "Am I on target?" "Am I flourishing? Have I designed my life so that I can flourish now, in every moment, as well as into the future?" This isn't about the finances. It's about living your life.

As you do this, you'll become aware of elements in your life that fall outside of your life plan. It becomes easier to say "no" to those elements that don't serve you. If you start to feel you've gone backwards, it is a perfect time to revisit the life planning exercises.

Living your life plan moves you from potential energy to kinetic energy. Its momentum continues to build propelling you forward. For many the movement is from a life of effort to one of vitality, joy, and ease.

When I redid my Three Questions recently, I discovered things that had never been in my life plan before. I went at fulfilling them with abandon. Shortly, I'd created a whole new workshop and realized a newfound passion for living a vigorous and vital life for many years.

The exercises will remind you of old passions and inspire new ones. That's what you want. You want to feel alive. Your life is yours.

What Could Possibly Get in the Way?

The classic obstacle to living our dream of freedom, the one we think of first, is money, so it was natural for me to help design the life planning field within financial services. I had been in the profession for several decades and could see that regardless of income, money wasn't the constraint to living a life of freedom. The constraint was one's self.

But what stunned me even more, and still to this day, was that when the dream was powerful and clear, nothing could get in its way. That's why we create the strongest possible vision in EVOKE. A weak torch and not believing we can accomplish it is what has always gotten in the way. When you craft your torch, it should light up the night sky.

So, if you find yourself not living the life you were meant to live, the very first thing to do is to see if the torch you have created for yourself is bright enough. Does it contain all the things you care about most? If it doesn't, put them all in! And then make sure the path to them is clear.

If they aren't exciting for you, how can you make them so? What would make your vision into a world you would be thrilled to live into? And are you giving yourself enough of the pleasure of it in a short enough time frame that you are motivated to put all your energy into making it happen? If not, dramatically shorten the time frame.

Domain Two: The Freedom of Life

Give yourself enough of your dream right now, or soon, that you are motivated and excited to be working to make your dream happen.

An example might be that you want to live in a cabin in the country but are tied to a city to make the money. If your goal is ten years away or more, you won't be nearly as motivated as you would be if you could find a way to get your dream home right now, or within a matter of months or a year or two. Think outside the box, if there are ways to make that happen, whether by remote work, or through a mortgage, or choosing your location better, or perhaps you could get the thrill of the experience by finding a way to live in the country for a month next year, two months the following year and all through the year after that.

Make your dream so palpable and exciting that you can't say "no" to it. And then imagine living in that dream. Take a couple of weeks and make it as real as can be to you. Make it live!

And if the dream is strong, but it's still a challenge, then list the obstacles, every one of them. Think creatively about each of them in order and in detail. You are on fire with your dream of freedom. What are the quickest solutions to each obstacle, the shortest path to your dream of freedom, so you can live the life you long to live right away? It's time to launch. You've just got this one life, why sacrifice the best years of it not living your dream, not making it both real and sustainable?

Money may be *an* obstacle, but it's not *the* obstacle. *The obstacle* is *you*. We often forget that money's purpose is to deliver us into our dream of freedom. Until we know what that dream is, we won't know the path to get there, and if we don't know the path, how can we craft a wise approach to money? Without a life plan, the ladder we're using to climb where we want to climb is very likely on the wrong wall.

Using the EVOKE process, financial life planners deliver their clients into their dream of freedom or to the passionate pursuit of their dream in a matter of weeks. You should do the same for yourself. These are dreams that might normally take 5, 10, 15, 20 years, 30 years to achieve. You might not be planning to get to them until you retire because you thought money was the constraint, and the torch wasn't bright. Or you might not get to them at all. For too many that is what happens. Money's not the constraint. The constraint is you. Put your focus where it is meant to be. It's time to get on with it. Your life is yours.

Another obstacle we often face is inadequate support from friends or family or professionals to guarantee we live our life plans.

If you decide to work with a financial life planner, you want to make sure the person you work with has the designations that have the highest levels of both financial skill and integrity.[6] You also want to know that they put you, as their client, first.[7] What's cool about people who are financial life planners is they've got the finances down and they're trained

---

[6] The CERTIFIED FINANCIAL PLANNER™ certification is a great place to begin, with their holistic approach to financial planning and their dedication to being fiduciaries to their clients.

[7] If I were looking for the highest integrity from a financial advisor, someone who puts me as their client first, I would seek out someone who 1) is a Registered Life Planner® professional, 2) is a fiduciary or CFP® practitioner, and 3) charges fee-only as opposed to fee-based or commissions. If you can't find all three in one person, two out of three is still pretty good.

in listening skills, empathy, and lighting the torch. It's all there, the complete package.

A financial planner trained in life planning is a fiduciary to their client. Though skilled in finance, they put their client's life first in their engagements.[8]

They serve you as a mentor and a champion. Someone who says, "You can do it," someone who can see the path before you and honors your ability to follow it, someone who says, "Let's make it happen and in short order!"

When you have someone, who knows money, that can sit there and say, "It ain't the money. Look, you can do this," and they nail your dream, money will no longer seem like an obstacle to you. You're ready to roll.

If you want to create your own life plan you can follow the prompts in this book or dive deeper into the process with my book *Life Planning for You: How to Design & Deliver the Life of Your Dreams* and the free website of the same name, *www.lifeplanningforyou.com*. They're a great starting point.

I've found it is most effective to do this process with another person at your side, or possibly a few other people. Just talking to someone about what you most long for in your life and hearing your dreams spoken back to you as both appropriate and fabulous, helps you move on them. If you have two or three friends who are allies around you living your dream, call them up and go forward.

---

[8] A fiduciary is an advisor who puts the client's interest ahead of their own. See *georgekinder.com* for my thoughts on the meaning and importance of fiduciary.

But be careful, too. Many people, even spouses, even people who love you, can dump a whole bucket of water on your dream of freedom. It's not that they're ill-meaning. They don't know any better. They aren't living their own dreams. Too often we fill our lives with cynicism, doubt, or distrust. Even if they support your dream and have the best of intentions, they are likely to pour some water on your dreams as their own fears around money arise.

What is required for this process to work best are people who you trust totally to be there for you for exactly what you want to deliver into the world. You'll know them. You know who they are, and you know if you don't have any. It's possible you don't.

I can think of three or four people in my life that are truly there for me. That's all. Of those people, none of them have the kind of training or the skills of a financially trained Registered Life Planner® (RLP®) professional. If you want someone who can put the whole picture together, you can find an RLP professional virtually anywhere, and because of our digital connectedness, virtually everywhere. In America, you can find someone in at least 42 of the 50 states. Internationally, they are in 15 countries from South Africa, to India, to Australia, to all over Europe. Many Registered Life Planner professionals work with clients over Zoom or other digital technology, in addition to face-to-face.

Another reason it's helpful to engage with a professional to guide you through the process is because they can offer you the accountability and support that often your best friends or family members can't.

Domain Two: The Freedom of Life

A financial life planner shared with me a story of one of her clients who was excited to finally redo her kitchen. She listened empathically as her client described the design and then they looked at how the $60,000 was lining up in her financial life plan. She recalled her client sharing in earlier meetings that spending more time with family was her number one priority. Her family was spread all over the country, all over the world. The financial life planner brought up the observation gently, "So when you did your Three Questions, family was most important, and now, we've got the kitchen. How is this going to impact your ability to deliver this dream of being more with the family?" They explored it, and it turns out that what meant more to her client was taking family vacations. She wanted to help fund a family vacation more than a kitchen and fund it once a year. She gained clarity through the process by revisiting her life plan with her planner and shifting from a money orientation to checking in with her heart.

The Three Questions are powerful. They have kept me on target throughout my life, to deliver what is most important into the world and in short order. Their importance has only grown over time as I have aged.

When I was a boy, I really wanted to sing. I wanted to write rock and roll songs and play the guitar. A lot of societal and family influences caused me to never pursue my dream. I was on other trajectories and doing well but that longing was still there. I had a nagging sense of disappointment for decades because I hadn't delivered this in my life.

I spent my first COVID summer with my wife and teenage daughters at our home in Massachusetts. We couldn't go anywhere, and I wanted to do a project with each of my daughters. My daughter London is quite musical and has a beautiful voice. I asked myself, "What could I do that would tap into some stuff for me, but would also really be tapping into what she's good at and what she loves to do?" I thought, "Maybe we could collaborate, maybe it's finally time to write those songs and perform them."

The world was spinning from the pandemic and from challenges to the environment, democracy, respect for each other, you name it. All over the world we were in a difficult place. I was upset and saw an opportunity to channel my feelings through song.

My daughter took on the task of the melody and the rhythm. I took on writing most of the lyrics. We overlapped; she pitched in with the lyrics some, and I pitched in some with the melodies. You can find our collaboration on Spotify and other streaming platforms as an album, *Shine Through*. It is filled with songs that capture what we were going through then: the timeless themes of democracy, the environment, and racism; the narcissism of dictators; and the challenges for people all over the world to live their lives in freedom. I catch myself singing one of the songs almost every day.

That summer I also began to take stock of my long COVID. I didn't know if I would get my vitality back and I knew that the dream at the heart of my third question might never be realized. It had a few answers in it, but always there were "living in the weather" and "illuminated manuscripts."

I had crafted my life to fulfill the dream of living in the weather and to be surrounded by nature. I spent much of my day attuned to nature's teachings, capturing its seasonal changes in poetry and photography. My quest was to understand the nature of the present moment by living it in nature, and to inspire others to do the same.

The books I'd wanted to deliver, these illuminated manuscripts, my nearly thirty years of work, were a ragged collection of 35,000 photographs and thousands of unedited pages of poetry. I found myself in tears one morning with my wife Kathy on the porch. What if I were to die with all my work unfinished?

I got to work with family and friends.

While London and I were composing *Shine Through*, her sister Rachel took time each day to help curate my 35,000 photos by calendar day and began the process of cropping and rating them for use in the book. I poured through poems and photographs, reviewing some of them for the first time in decades, searching for the best reflections of the present moment, revising many, and making sure there were images and words for each day of the year.

With help from my team at Kinder Institute, the first of five books, *Reflections on Spectacle Pond: The Weekly Edition* was released in a digital version in December 2021, capturing in over 50 two-page spreads, photography and poetry for each week of the year. Shortly thereafter *The Daily Editions* followed the individual seasons day-by-day.

All in all, nearly a thousand poems and photographs in five books were published digitally,[9] completed under the duress of long COVID, in just two years. Though they may mean little to others, to me they are my legacy. I think of them as

---

9 A free version of *Reflections on Spectacle Pond: Weekly and Daily Editions* is available by subscription at georgekinder.com.

a contemporary *Book of Hours*, a meditative guide outlining a path to live in nature and in the present moment. Without the clarity and urgency that came from my third question, I doubt if the work would ever have been done.

Because of the Three Questions, I've put my passionate pursuits first, ahead of everything. Everything. It has meant for me that I flourish more than I ever imagined possible. And if instead I find myself in a funk, I have immediate access to the Three Domains of Freedom, each of them a path that transforms suffering into wisdom.

Nothing gets in the way of a blazing torch.

Nothing.

Your life is yours.

What Happens If We All Do It?

Not a single person who has come to me for life planning was living a perfectly fulfilled life. There was still something, often many things, they aspired to deliver into the world. The financial life planners that I trained found the same thing with their clients. Imagine if that's happening across society, what energy, potential, good-heartedness, innovative spirit, kindness, and integrity we are missing as a civilization? It's mind-boggling.

If society was based upon the Second Domain of Freedom, the principle that your life is yours, and we all lived that freedom, we would find a world more entrepreneurial than we have ever imagined.

Right now, our world is driven by a tiny hierarchy of all the possible entrepreneurial energy out there. A handful of people are given the gifts of great venture capital, private equity, and the enormous resources that follow. Just a handful. Imagine if instead everyone was alive with entrepreneurial fervor from living their life plan. Entrepreneurial spirit would be everywhere. In every corner of our lives, the world would be blossoming with innovations of spirit, of community, of kindness, as well as of our material needs as a people, as a species, and as a planet.

Innovations that would end corruption, bring authenticity and creativity into all aspects of our lives, and establish a civilization of integrity for generations to come would blossom forth.

Too much, we think of growth as economic, but that is such a small measure of human progress. I don't measure growth by money. I measure it by how much energy I'm putting into the world, I measure it by how much kindness we can all feel around us, how much we experience the human beings around us working together to make the world a better place. This is what the Second Domain of Freedom delivers.

We are living a pittance of our potential, far less than what each of us could be adding to the world. The vitality that we have our children benefit from, as do our children's children. Instead, we squirrel away so much of the energy of human beings into structures of lethargy, cynicism, helplessness, addictions, and doubt inside us and into inefficient and anachronistic hierarchies of power outside of us that now deliver a planet that's in danger, democracies that are threatened, with corruption, war, violence, bigotry, racism, and propaganda mushrooming like a fungus from darkness deep inside, taking our lives and our spirits away.

There are two reasons it is important to begin living your purpose every day of your life: The first is personal and the second is societal.

When you're not living your purpose, you're only working at half speed, as if you were breathing only half the oxygen you need. We accomplish so much more when we're aligned with our purpose. We are both at ease and on fire because we are delivering who we are authentically into the world. We thrive and flourish when we are fulfilling who we are.

Our lives become far more efficient because we no longer live under clouds of woulda-shoulda-coulda. We're doing it.

We think of ourselves as a high-growth society. We are not, or everybody would be firing on all cylinders. The problem is not necessarily intentional, but it is societal. Our parents said we couldn't, or it was our spouse, or our friends, co-workers, neighbors, or our theories of markets and the bosses and hierarchies of power that control them. All the people around us have their own ideas of what we should be doing. We internalize their messages and start living our lives for them, instead of for ourselves. They may not intend to do this, but it's happening, and it's holding us back as a society. It is a simple thing to fix.

Now, just imagine that everyone understood their passionate purpose and had the resources and encouragement to claim the Second Domain of Freedom and to live the lives they want. That's the world I want to live in. It's time to deliver it.

Some say there are a thousand great entrepreneurs in the world today, some say there are 500 million. I think there are eight billion of us. Life planning was designed to free us all.

It's time for us. Let's live our lives and show the world what living lives of freedom can bring. Your life is yours. It's time to live it.

Conclusion

Your Life is Yours. Putting the Freedom of Moments into the Freedom of Your Life.

I always keep my answers to the third question in front of me. Revisiting them gives me the confidence that I am going for them or am already living them. It means everything.

When we live in the Second Domain of Freedom, we wake up each morning excited to be alive, thrilled to be delivering our lives exactly as we have chosen into the world.

There's a relationship between the first and second domains of freedom. In the first, each moment of your life is a domain of freedom, and you can access that freedom any time you want. In each of these moments, you are free of self. From there it is easy to tap into any virtue you need as well as to the great energy that delivers what you want into the world. That energy becomes turbo-charged in Domain Two, where it links to your passionate purpose. It extends into the future with the vision of who you want to be.

The freedom of moments strengthens the second domain by giving you access to great courage and the focus required for what you want in life. You find more patience and equanimity in the times you aren't quite able to do what you want, or when you need more time to achieve your goal.

Domain Two: The Freedom of Life

The first domain provides resilience to deliver the second because in each moment we can find ourselves, our authenticity, who we really are. We're living the life we're meant to live. We understand intrinsically that our life is ours.

At the same time, the second domain, where we claim our lives as our own, bolsters the first domain by surrounding it with so much authenticity, happiness, and fulfillment that in any moment you can more easily find your presence.

When you realize the first two domains of freedom, each of the tasks and responsibilities that lie like a tapestry over those moments is filled with the joy of being your path to freedom.

Not only is each moment yours, but your life is yours.

Next, we will see how civilization is yours, linking all our freedoms together in community.

Domain Three:

The Freedom of Civilization. All Creatures Meant to Be Free.

Civilization is our place of community, of kindness, of creativity and joy, of freedom and exchange. It is who we are.

Introduction

Civilization is who we are, as a people, as a species.

It is everywhere we go and every place we visit. It is this whole human enterprise, from our buildings to our fields, from our industries to our mom-and-pop shops. It is everything humans are and everything we create.

Each day we build civilization in what we do, just as our ancestors did for thousands of years before us and as our descendants will continue to do when we have passed.

It doesn't matter if we live in poverty or in wealth. It doesn't matter the degree of privilege or its absence in our lives.

Domain Three: The Freedom of Civilization

Civilization becomes a domain of freedom when it is nourished by our authenticity, by who we are at our best, when we act from the first two domains of freedom, claiming each moment as ours and our lives as ours.

I'm not talking utopia. Rather, civilization as a domain of freedom is the initial phase of a sustainable civilization, a sustainable species of *Homo sapiens*, a species that will continue to evolve as civilization itself evolves, because that is who we are.

You may be wondering, as you consider the freedom of civilization, what power does one person out of eight billion have? And how can we bring freedom to people all over the world who lack it?

In my youth, I wanted to choose to live in freedom wherever I went, but the great rushing river of civilization was too powerful and swept me into its own current instead. I felt I had no choice. I must follow its way or drown in its flood. I have been disappointed that civilization offered so few paths to freedom. Even with the privileges of birth and education that I had, I felt an inability to manifest my own destiny. How true this must be for most of humanity. But things have changed, both for me and for the world. From my own struggles, and in the midst of great doubt, watching both the wonders and the horrors of life, I found a way to make civilization a domain of freedom. I'd like to share it with you.

From the first two domains of freedom, I learned that the negative, the obstacles, the darkness, are gifts. Each of them reveals a "future" for us to discover, or to uncover, that delivers freedom, our authenticity into the nature of civilization, seeding civilization with freedom.

The struggles of the planet and its peoples are our own. The polarization of politics, distrust of neighbors, and fear of the future are their consequences and manifestations. They are the places to which we are called. Our ancestral communities that could successfully govern themselves while living sustainably with the Earth are a thing of the past, if they ever existed.

In a civilization of freedom, we are called to be leaders, each of us, not to follow, unless what we follow models our own best nature. Although we may already lead in our communities, something shifted in the world as this last millennium moved to the next. Each of us finds ourselves connected to all of Gaia,[10] in the historical blink of an eye, whether by our pollution, by our democracies, or by our smart phones. Beyond our communities, it is time for us to insist on a moral vision for all of humanity, a moral vision that includes all of Gaia, a standard for civilization that is modeled by every institution, every hierarchy of power, every corporation, nonprofit, and government. For the powers that we, the people, grant them, it is time we held them all to a higher standard.

Today, civilization is filled with nations claiming their space as democracies. More people will vote in the year I am completing this book, 2024, than in any previous year in history, though for many their votes are marred by corruption in media and politics. Some nations have great freedoms for their people, human and humane rights.

---

10   Gaia was a goddess of the earth in ancient Greece. Now (from Merriam-Webster), it is "the hypothesis that the living and nonliving components of Earth function as a single system in such a way that the living component regulates and maintains conditions (such as the temperature of the ocean or composition of the atmosphere) so as to be suitable for life."

Domain Three: The Freedom of Civilization

Many of them, abusing truth and both the language of democracy and the people that speak it, support autocracy, dictatorships or oligarchies that obscure and stand in the way of democratic freedoms. Regardless of what is happening around you and the state of your nation, civilization is yours. It is your Third Domain of Freedom.

Each of us is a part of civilization. We are meant to deliver its freedoms to all, creating new liberties and expanding old ones. The freedom of civilization is both to live in its freedoms and to deliver them to others. The freedom to speak, to determine who governs us, to trust the laws or the systems to which we are subject – or to work to change them.

For civilization to be a domain of freedom, we must learn the power and dignity and integrity of standing alone in this world and the great joy of standing with others. Whichever it happens to be, this domain of freedom can only be fully created by us.

All over the world people are suffering. The planet burns and many species are lost; corruption and wars proliferate; *Homo sapiens* themselves may not survive; democracy is fragile. Without the best of humanity at its core, civilization is unsustainable.

It is time to speak our truth, yours and mine. We are the voice of the Earth. Gaia speaks through us, through the best of us, through our authenticity, our kindness, and our truth. Our meanness is not sustainable. It is time for the Earth and all its creatures to flourish.

We must be ashamed when we see corruption or pollution, war or the abuse of power. We must immediately speak out, persistently and publicly. Civilization is ours. It is time to put to an end these acts of violence against our humanity.

For civilization to endure, much less to thrive, we must embrace it as our own. Not to be conquered, it is our family. We have the power to make it one of freedom and of a kindness that takes care of all. We are the only species that can contemplate and care for all of Gaia's creatures. No other species on the planet has that power or that responsibility. Let us not squander it.

Democracy is civilization's standard for claiming freedoms within it. In the First Domain of Freedom, living in the moment connects us through our sensations ("listening" to them) to the environment that surrounds us, and to the transformational power of change. Likewise, in democracy, listening with an open heart to each other creates a civilization that is natural and organic, humane, and filled with freedom. Through democracy, we celebrate the freedoms we experience and are naturally inclined to extend them to others.

Civilization is yours, this network of engagement between you and all that surrounds you. It's a domain of freedom. And you create it. Each of us creates it.

Let's look at how this is done. In this next section, we will explore how to make civilization a domain of freedom, how to live as if it already was a domain of freedom, and how to create a practice of engagement within civilization.

The Practice

How do you live in the freedom of civilization? How do you make civilization yours?

People say, what is the sense of our small effort? They cannot see that we must lay one brick at a time, take one step at a time. A pebble cast into a pond causes ripples that spread in all directions. Each one of our thoughts, words and deeds is like that. No one has a right to sit down and feel hopeless. There is too much work to do.

— **Dorothy Day**

Never doubt that a small group of thoughtful, committed citizens can change the world: indeed, it's the only thing that ever has.

— **Margaret Mead**

My actions are my only true belongings. I cannot escape the consequences of my actions. My actions are the ground on which I stand.

— **Thich Nhat Hanh**

Many practices help us gain the freedom of civilization. I'll focus on two, but there are as many as there are people to imagine them. In this section, I will emphasize living in civilization as a domain of freedom, as an experience of celebration and joy. I will also focus on how we can bring compassion, kindness, and a spirit of innovation to everything we do.

It starts with your presence, with your living into the dream and then acting to make it happen everywhere. As you act you will naturally gather community around you. So, to begin,

1. Celebrate the spirit of The Third Domain of Freedom as if you were already living it. Celebrate your authenticity, your virtue and awakening, as both the experience and the establishment of civilization, as your domain of freedom.

2. Proclaim to others that civilization is meant to be a domain of freedom and proclaim your intention to make it so. Proclaim that each of us is here to make civilization a domain of freedom. Hold others accountable, particularly our institutions, our hierarchies, and now, Artificial Intelligence (AI).

As great as the challenges are for us in Domains One and Two, the results of our actions there manifest quickly. More is required of us in Domain Three, where, though we care deeply we must act without expectation of success, merely because it is right and because it arises naturally from our authenticity or our virtue.

The first two domains of freedom give us great strength. Harnessing their enormous creative energy, we apply it meticulously to all of civilization. It is the energy of awakening: the awakening of a moment, the awakening of a life, and the awakening of civilization.

Without the Third Domain of Freedom, the first and second domains are unsustainable. Without the first and second domains, the third is unimaginable.

Domain Three: The Freedom of Civilization

Among the most powerful actions we can take is to insist that all hierarchies of power treat each of us with respect and humanity. It is time to establish this as a right, for all of us, to live in a world that is trustworthy in all its institutions. Here are some of the practices that give civilization the vitality of a domain of freedom for each of us right now.

> *<u>Celebrate</u> every day the ways civilization already is a domain of freedom. Celebrate your freedoms of speech and action.*
>
> *<u>Experience Freedom in Every Moment, Live in Freedom.</u> Freedom is not a "to do" list. If we do not live life as freedom, open-hearted as we engage, our actions in civilization will be flawed and deliver darkness rather than light.*
>
> *<u>Design</u> pathways in every engagement you have that will work for the freedom of all beings. Gather with others in each of the institutions within which you participate to think about the whole organization. It is important to join as people first and as an institution second when considering change that is systemic, so that the civilization that arises is organic, authentic, trustworthy, sustainable, and humane.*
>
> *<u>Deliver</u>, as a fiduciary, the freedoms that you create, including, within your own job, the trustworthiness that consumers and communities require to live in freedom. Remind yourself of the value of spreading virtues across the planet, even, and perhaps especially, to the very next person you meet.*

Claim your Freedom, Pursue it. It is in understanding your own passion for freedom that you can contribute the most to civilization. No one else will know it quite as well as you. Pursuing your own freedom may feel selfish, but it paves the way for others to live in theirs.

Create and Deliver Freedom to Others. With creativity, vitality, kindness, and courage, act to create a world that maximizes freedom for all. Proclaim to others that it is time to end corruption, war, and falsehoods from our institutions, to end pollution and to establish trustworthiness as the law of the land. Speak truth to power. Bring kindness to people. Join movements. Run for office. Vote.

Celebration

One of the books that I keep two versions of, one by my bedside table and the other at my writing desk, is *The Analects of Confucius*. I've read them dozens of times. I love them because they're very simple, and they have been with me since the beginning of my reflections on the failures of civilization.

Confucius was wrestling with corruption that plagued the warring states of China during his lifetime. He aspired to create a society of virtue, profoundly believing that a great civilization was crafted of great human beings.

In one story, the ruler of one of the states of China complained to Confucius about the greedy, thieving nature of his people. Confucius simply replied if you stop your own greed and thieving of people, they will all model themselves after you and follow you.

In another story, he said, "You know I love virtue. But the truth is, you can search 10 houses around here and you'll find someone who loves virtue as much as I do." I thought all right, so lots of people appreciate virtue. He then said, "But you'd have to search a thousand homes to find someone who loves learning as much as I do."

When we value all the cultural and scientific learning that is passed down through generations, it is a way that we build civilization as structures of freedom for all to enjoy. Confucius was ahead of his time in understanding that.

He went further and said, "The greatest thing I've learned is that loving is better than learning." Loving is the bond that holds civilization together. But he didn't stop there, he went on to say, "And rejoicing is better than loving." And that's the key. We need to rejoice in civilization, in this whole amazing world that we've been born into. It is in rejoicing that we experience the freedom of civilization, and it is from our rejoicing that we can create a civilization for all that is better than any that has ever been experienced in the past.

When we listen to others, respectfully, even humbly, from the place of celebration, something amazing happens. They are less threatened by us, and we feel less threatened by them. Instead, we make civilization together.

Live as if the freedom of civilization is already here, live in celebration and kindness. Civilization is "who we are" – at our best – all of us, awakened and kind.

All Creatures Meant to be Free

Ninety percent of the world's population now owns a smart phone, with health and how-to information and world-class libraries, music, weather, maps, and travel information at their fingertips. In developed countries, most of us have freedoms of information, communication, and democracy. We have the power to vote, freedom of assembly, of speech, and of the press. Though in many places those freedoms are limited or do not exist, nearly all human beings recognize the value of these freedoms. Where we may not be living up to the standard of the Third Domain of Freedom, we have all the information necessary and the ability to make it happen. In some places it will be more difficult than others. Coming together, all over the world, we can make it happen everywhere.

The poet Walt Whitman celebrated each of our contributions to make America a great new "democratic vista." It's time to reawaken that sense of celebration without undermining or ignoring the hard work that remains. Rather, let's use celebration to invigorate our actions. By recognizing the brilliance and vitality that people have put into innovating, collaborating, and influencing what the best of civilization has become, we honor them as we catalog for ourselves what *is* working so well, and what isn't yet accomplished.

I practice daily living in a state of celebration. I allow myself to live into each experience of appreciation, gratitude, and wonder that comes my way. For a moment, I pause with it and allow myself to be that experience, allowing it to fill my life with joy, no matter how ordinary or seemingly insignificant.

In recent years, many of us experienced illness during the pandemic and are unhappy with the turmoil in the world.

Knowing that we have hospitals that can keep us alive and a supportive community that can take care of us when we are ill is worth celebrating. For many of us there's a safety net. And where there isn't or it is inadequate, we can support the changes that are necessary to establish one and celebrate that. Civilization is not always and in all ways a domain of freedom. We make it that way with practice.

A celebration mindset helps us to be more thoughtful, collaborative, and creative in times of challenge. It's also a lot of fun. It's like being part of the biggest party on Earth. There's always something to celebrate. Often, it's right next to something that makes you somber, something to make better.

The Three Domains of Freedom belong to everyone. For me, the freedom of civilization is to bring the Three Domains of Freedom to everyone, everywhere. My commitment to do that is something I celebrate.

To cultivate a mind of celebration, I encourage you to keep a daily log of at least one thing that is worth celebrating and one way that you have furthered the freedoms of civilization. Keep the notebook by your bedside and each night write your celebration or do it each morning as you wake. Write anything that you experience or notice. Something that makes you appreciate civilization or what it has done for you.

In this diary, I like to capture the very best moment of each day of my life. I write it as a recollection, a haiku, a prayer of gratitude, or a story, and at the end, I list something that civilization created that contributed to my ability to have that experience. I have made my diary something of a legacy journal, a record of the best moments of my life, something, perhaps, my grandchildren will love to read.

Join me in celebrating what we have.

Once we know our freedom to celebrate civilization, we gain the vitality and inspiration to pursue greater freedoms for ourselves and others within civilization.

Making it Happen

There are many ways for us to create, design, and deliver a civilization of freedom for all. It requires many hands. Where we see something that needs to be done or that we can do, we pitch in. Part of the freedom of civilization is that we create it as we live it. And as we create it, we are trailblazers, establishing paths for others to experience similar or greater freedoms as ourselves. These pathways become *environments of freedom*, where all people thrive.

Democracy is an example of an environment of freedom that makes ever greater freedoms possible.

In addition to the rights we already have, it is time for another great environment of freedom to be added to our rights. It is time for us to require our institutions to be trustworthy. It should be the right of all human beings to expect every institution they engage with to be trustworthy in everything they say and do. I call the proposal to secure this right Fiduciary In All Things or FIAT.

Nothing can make our institutions human, but FIAT guarantees that they will be humane.

In an accomplished civilization, one that is truly a domain of freedom, FIAT is baked in. A civilization that delivers itself to all as a domain of freedom, is a fiduciary civilization. It is fiduciary in all things. It creates a sustainable civilization of freedoms, now and for generations to come.

Fiduciary In All Things (FIAT): It's Origins

We have it in our power to begin the world over again.

— *Thomas Paine*

I have been concerned for some time about the state of humanity. The feeling has increased over the last ten years. I am concerned about the things that I care about most, like how we treat each other, the vast inequalities amongst human beings, the state of Mother Earth, democracy, and perhaps most important of all I am concerned about misrepresentations of the truth by those in power, those whom we should most trust in the community we call civilization.

Coming out of the banking crisis of 2008, I suspected that although humanity seemed to be polarized, perhaps, in truth, everyone was concerned about the same things. And that we mostly wanted the same solutions. This idea launched my book, *A Golden Civilization & The Map of Mindfulness*, and a book tour to far corners of the globe. As I traveled, I was searching for how to create a vision strong enough that the whole world would act on it. To test my intuition, wherever I went I invited audiences through a structured exercise, to design their own vision of a Golden Civilization.[11]

Sure enough, whether I went to a rich country or to a poor country, and whether I went to a democratic country or a dictatorship or somewhere in between, everywhere people wanted similar things. Everybody wanted less inequality. They wanted adequate healthcare, food, and shelter. They wanted an end to corruption. They wanted an end to racism and to bigotry. They wanted kindness and good humor. They wanted a richness of culture. They wanted to be able to trust their scientists. They wanted trustworthiness everywhere. They wanted all media to tell the truth and to be trustworthy. This discovery was quite wonderful.

I captured the vision words, weighted by frequency of use, from the first 20 conversations into a word-cloud shaped like the Earth.

---

11   Learn about the Golden Civilization Conversations including how to host them yourself by visiting georgekinder.com and selecting "A Golden Civilization."

Figure 2. Golden Civilization Conversations Word Cloud

Vision words weighted by the frequency that they came up in conversation during the first 20 Golden Civilization Conversations led by George Kinder around the globe.

How self-centered we have been playing one country versus another, one team versus another, one person versus another. For generations, we've lived with the notion that evolution is about competition, but it's much more clearly about Gaia and the creation of expanding environments of freedom. As the world becomes smaller and more accessible to us, it becomes our responsibility to create environments where all creatures thrive. We are being called as a species to deliver a structure of kindness, freedom, innovation, compassion, resilience, and sustainability for the whole Earth, for our descendants, and for all generations to come.

What does that look like?

How do we begin?

What is the vision?

◇◇◇◇◇◇◇◇◇◇◇◇

As I reflected on these experiences, I began a search for the simplest of pathways to create a Golden Civilization across the world. Having minored in economics at Harvard, I made a point of taking time each year to study the theories of the latest Nobel Prize winners. I revisited some of the economic thinking I had learned.

250 years ago, at the beginning of the Industrial Revolution, there was an explosion of innovation, of creativity, and of the production of material things that would lead humanity to create the world we are now in, enabling many of us to live longer, healthier, and richer lives and be connected to each other all over the world.

Clearly, the combination of capitalism, democracy, and the rule of law produced something remarkable, bringing to much of humanity greater longevity, greater leisure, and greater freedoms. But if our system was really the best that there could be, why is it that at the top of every hierarchy of power after these 250 years of innovation, we don't find the very best of humanity, our wisdom and our compassion? Wouldn't the best system automatically deliver the very best of humanity into every aspect of our lives?

Something at the very base of the system is awry in the design of every organizational structure, something that keeps each institution from acting automatically with wisdom and kindness, so much so that no institution anywhere models it. We are back to the model of competition, where self-interest comes first. Our institutional structures are designed for self-interest to flourish. Rather than virtuous action, it's self-interest that's baked in.

Think about it. When we give the right to incorporate or the right to govern to a person or an organization, we give the potential for enormous power. And they can leverage that power through hierarchy, minimize the threat of lawsuits with limited liability protection, and get special tax rates. They can further leverage their power to astronomical levels with capital and debt and through their ability to communicate. With all this power at their fingertips, is it any wonder that the production and delivery of humanity's innovations, although they touch every aspect of our lives, is more tainted by the self-interest of hierarchies than touched by human virtue?

For all the power we have granted their self-interest, why don't we require something of them in return? What if we simply required each of them as a consequence of incorporation, whether they are corporations, nonprofits, or governments, to act in a humane way? Simply require them to be humane.

But rather than require something of them, we keep giving more to them. After thousands of years of developing what it is to have secured rights as human beings in relation to the powerful institutions that govern our lives, we've granted a lot of those rights back to institutions as if they were human. We have granted them the power to dominate how we think through their ownership or influence of media, including through non-profits and their own advertising. And we've granted them the enormous power to influence elections in ways that takes away our democratic freedom.

Only now do we realize that in using those rights, some of the most powerful have come to threaten our deepest values, our lives, our democracies, the lives of Earth's creatures, and the stability of the planet we live on. We feel diminished, as if civilization is not ours but our institutions'. But civilization is ours. It is meant to be a domain of freedom, not for them but for us.

It's time we asked new and existing institutions (corporate, non-profit, governmental) to place humanity first, to place the truth first, to place democracy first, and to place the Earth first ahead of their own self-interest, as a requirement of their existence. This is the essence of the FIAT movement.

Here is the simple, one-sentence legislative proposal that requires just that.

> *"A Fiduciary standard of obligation is required for all institutions (corporate, non-profit, and governmental) to place the interests of all stakeholders, of truth, of humanity, democracy, and the living planet that sustains us, first above their own self-interest."*

We fought a revolution in America for democracy, to establish human rights, and to free ourselves of the hierarchy of mad King George. But now, as a consequence of our system, we have created many hierarchies as powerful and more. It is time for us as a species to free the world as well as ourselves of the hierarchies that have power over us and that can diminish our freedom and guarantee instead that each of them always works in the best interests of humanity.

This simple piece of legislation will make sure this happens. The idea and the language are simple enough to spread across the globe. Through speaking engagements, I've shared these ideas, reaching many parts of the world. It's easy to think of obstacles to the accomplishing of such a human right, but at this stage, it's the vision that's most important to establish. A strong enough vision will conquer all obstacles, particularly when it's the movement of a people, a species, inspired by the same torch.

With the richest and most powerful billionaires, companies, and media moguls likely to oppose placing the interests of truth, democracy, Mother Earth, and humanity above their own self-interest, it is imperative we create a huge grass-roots movement toward Fiduciary In All Things becoming the law of the land.

Many who first hear the idea don't understand what the word "fiduciary" means, and to some it can seem controversial. I chose the term "fiduciary" because of its linguistic roots and its legislative usage. Fiduciary is an obligation for trustworthy service to others.

At present all corporations have a single fiduciary responsibility. It is to their shareholders. All the power of their hierarchy and leverage is required to maximize profit for their shareholders alone. That is the nub of our problem. For a civilization to be a domain of freedom for all, hierarchies of power must have a fiduciary responsibility to all of us, and to truth and to Gaia and democracy, as well.

I've been sharing simple statements to help bridge the gap between the term fiduciary and its meaning.

- We need a standard for humanity.
- We need a standard for humanity that is trustworthy in all things.
- Every institution we create must be trustworthy in all things, no exceptions.
- Fiduciary means trustworthy.
- Fiduciary is the legal term for trustworthy service to others, placing their interest always above one's own.
- A one-sentence legislative proposal could change the world.
- A fiduciary standard of obligation is required for all institutions, corporate, nonprofit, governmental, to place the interests of all stakeholders, of truth, of humanity, democracy, and the living planet that sustains us first above their own self-interest.
- Trustworthy institutions as fiduciaries to us all tell the truth, the whole truth, and nothing but the truth in all communications.
- Trustworthy institutions as fiduciaries to us all put the health of democracy and Mother Earth above their own self-interest.
- Let's make fiduciary and the trustworthiness of our institutions the law of the land.

Even more accessible than words for a movement to go viral are images.

In the United States, consumers can find a Certified Organic symbol on any organically processed food that is certified by the USDA. This simple symbol indicates to a consumer

Domain Three: The Freedom of Civilization

that the product has fulfilled conditions on how they are produced, processed, transported, and stored.

For the Fiduciary In All Things movement, I've created easily recognizable symbols that can go on an organization's website to symbolize that they care about the humane treatment of their employees, of democracy, and of the living planet that sustains them.

> A one-sentence legislative proposal:
>
> *"A Fiduciary standard of obligation is required for all institutions (corporate, non-profit, and governmental) to place the interests of all stakeholders, of truth, of humanity, democracy, and the living planet that sustains us, first above their own self-interest."*
>
> I support making FIDUCIARY IN ALL THINGS the law of the land
> www.FiduciaryInAllThings.com

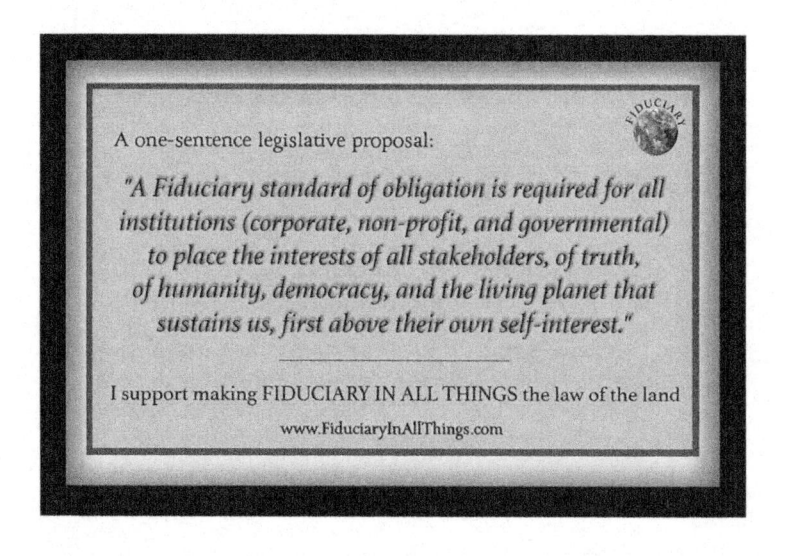

Figure 3. Fiduciary In All Things Legislative Proposal

A one-sentence legislative proposal crafted by George Kinder that advocates for all institutions to place the interests of all stakeholders above their own self-interest.

www.FiduciaryInAllThings.com

Figure 4. Fiduciary In All Things Globe Logo

A logo that can help spread awareness of the FIAT movement by adding it to your social media posts, websites, headers, and email signatures.

Figure 5. Fiduciary In All Things Square Logo

A logo that can help spread awareness of the FIAT movement by adding it to your social media posts, websites, headers, and email signatures.

You can popularize these symbols by sharing them on social media and placing them on your website and in your communications to demonstrate your support of the vision of a fiduciary world.

We have a strong vision. Let's spread it widely. I'm optimistic that we can do this, despite those of enormous wealth and power that would prefer institutions to work solely for them. Already there are significant existing structures that can support the implementation of legislation. They come from the ESG movement, Business Roundtable, B Corps, and many organizations and corporations looking to put humanity's interests ahead of their own self-interest. Extraordinarily helpful as each of these may be, at this point, establishing the vision is even more important than solving obstacles. It's time to make Fiduciary In All Things the law of the land, by making its vision ubiquitous and for all people.

Imagine all people of the Earth empowered, supported, and inspired, not diminished by the systems that surround them. Just a single sentence legislative proposal can start this and can change the world. Let's establish the vision. We need all hands on deck. Please join us. Share what #FiduciaryInAllThings means to you. Place the symbols on your social media headers and banners, and on your website. Let's make it happen.

Consider these questions:

- *What is it that you can do to popularize Fiduciary In All Things across your networks, including through political and service organizations?*

- *What are some possible challenges that this movement could face? How might we overcome them?*

- *What are some speaking engagements, small or large, that you could arrange to help spread FIAT?*

Speaking Truth to Power, Bring Kindness to People

Moderation in temper is always a virtue; but moderation in principle is always a vice.
— **Thomas Paine**

Truth and kindness are the foundations of a Golden Civilization. FIAT is an expression of both. When we speak truth to power, we help create a fiduciary responsibility toward humanity within our institutions. If we don't speak it, only those at the top of the hierarchies thrive.

The Three Domains of Freedom are the field of dignity and kindness out of which speaking truth to power springs. Civilization is ours. Where it does harm, let yourself be outraged. Channel your anger into the dignity that brings courtesy and kindness to people and speaks truth to power. You are claiming civilization as a domain of freedom and modeling how it is so.

We will need all of us working together to make this successful. The more people are engaged, the more truthful civilization becomes. All institutions must be accountable for the words they utter, for the political contributions they make, for the non-profits they support. And the banks that lend them money must be accountable as well.

For those in war or political persecution there are times when to be free in civilization means to hide out, to be someone no one sees, to do the work of truth and kindness and freedom quietly.

And there are times when to be free in civilization requires one to shine through the most horrible situation, through deprivations of hunger and torture and worse.

In all circumstances, civilization is our Third Domain of Freedom. Here we are meant to be free and to bring freedom to all others. If we don't, who will?

So many things require global attention. The fact that they haven't yet been addressed often means that there hasn't been enough truth spoken. Civilization needs you. All people must speak up if our voices are to be heard.

Speaking truth to power is challenging. Often, we find ourselves speaking from the voice of a victim, rather than from one already free. The institutions themselves facilitate this experience. We need courage, but it also helps to find allies and communities that are already concerned or engaged in creating their own versions of a Golden Civilization.

At this moment, the most important truth to power that we can speak of is that it is time to create a Golden Civilization, one that ends corruption, establishes democracy, and brings freedom everywhere. And that we are all eager and engaged to contribute to making this happen as we claim our third domain of freedom, the freedom of civilization. There is no excuse any more for war or propaganda, for corruption or bigotry or violence. "One Earth, one family, one future" was the theme of the G20 summit in 2023. The phrase was derived from the Upanishads, thousands of years old. Its time has come.

And equally important, if anything could be, it is time to insist that every hierarchy of power is responsible in every form of media to speak the Truth, the Whole Truth, and Nothing but the Truth.

What Else Can We Do? What Other Action Can We Take?

Given the crises we experience on the planet, it is important to dedicate time each day to living the freedom of civilization and to delivering it. I suggest spending some time, perhaps 10-30 minutes a day, to consciously engage in the world. It might mean engaging in politics or simply being aware in your place of work how you make a difference. Where there are flaws, initiate conversations that deliver solutions.

It may not be obvious where you'd like to engage, what you'd like to change or to do. Take a bit of time to find where you can be creative and take responsibility for civilization. Pick something that's important to you. It could be local or national. It might feel urgent, be something you are passionate about, or it might be something that lends itself to skills you have mastered. Form a habit around the practice of engaging with civilization for 10-30 minutes each day, just as you've done to establish your mindfulness practice.

As part of your life planning third question, what political or civilizational change to the world or your country or your community would give you a thrill to see happen? How could you help? On a weekly or daily basis? On a yearly basis? What vigorous action could you take?

Domain Three: The Freedom of Civilization

I can think of several changes that I am committed to delivering:

1. To bring Democracy everywhere. An action step would be to work to strengthen it in America, where I live.
2. To safeguard the Earth and its species. A step would be to familiarize environmental groups with the FIAT standard.
3. To make certain FIAT is built into all AI decision making, to guarantee that AI is committed to creating a Golden Civilization in short order, and to establishing it in all institutions as a foundational principle.

Here are some questions to consider:

- *Where does civilization not live up to your values?*
- *What is the issue that you're most passionate about that you want to deliver on, both globally and locally?*
- *What is the issue that you feel is most urgent? How could you help to address it?*
- *Where might you use your skills to have the most impact, locally or globally?*
- *How can you focus on civilization daily? Is there a time or a place where you can bring your focus to bear?*
- *Are there communities that can support the work you want to do? How might you engage with them?*

Establishing civilization as a domain of freedom is like landing the first man on the moon, or ending apartheid in

South Africa, something we thought was impossible, until we got the will and the gumption to do it. But this time, it's on all of us, not just enlightened nations, to bring a Golden Civilization into being.

What Could Possibly Get in the Way?

Freedom is the continuous action we all must take, and each generation must do its part, to create an even more fair, more just society.

— *John Lewis*

We won't even see it, the elephant in the room. We'll not quite get that things are not ok, that democracy may die, and the Earth with it. Instead, while it's happening, we'll believe the emperors as they describe their new clothes. After all, who other than emperors have access to and veto power over what we read and see in the media and the power to alter it with AI.

Our ignorance, fed by complacency, by our doubt and discouragement, will get in the way. False notions already dominate our minds; especially the belief that civilization is not ours but belongs to hordes of others out there, or to our emperors, bosses, and kings, and we can do little about it.

There's a reason greed and fear top the list of inner obstacles I heard in Golden Civilization Conversations. In the face of great inequality, it feels natural to blame the greed of others and feel like a victim, powerless and fearful in a world without freedom, co-dependent with institutions that all seem one up on us. After all, where a corporation has a freedom of speech that is millions of times more powerful than ours is, then what's the meaning of our freedom of speech?

So, we huddle in front of the TV for hours, scroll on our smartphones, or divert and diminish our endeavors through alcohol and drugs. If we do act it might be by saying something nasty to someone with different viewpoints or a different background or identity, or by harming them physically or emotionally.

Even with the first two domains of freedoms surging inside us, we still require the sustainable freedom of civilization if we are to be free. But mostly we get in our own way, colluding unwittingly with those in power. They don't want us to take action, or to see how they are thriving at our expense and at the expense of our world. So instead, our world is filled with the optimistic or polarizing voices of those in power and the lethargy of those (like sheep) without. It's time to permanently end this.

◇◇◇◇◇◇◇◇◇◇◇

And then there are the world's obstacles – one of the most wonderful things about this domain of freedom. As challenging as they seem, they are our ground. Though they seem much greater than the obstacles of the First and Second Domains of Freedom, as my father used to say, "the bigger they are, the harder they fall." And it's time to bring them down.

Although real victory doesn't happen overnight, it's best to act as if everything you do makes a difference, knowing that a healthy Earth, a strong democracy, and a free people will make a difference for millennia to come. When you act from the standpoint of freedom, you immediately gain that freedom, and a vitality you can get in no other way! You model it for others, all of us building civilization as a domain of freedom for everyone we know.

The challenges are huge, though what seems even more challenging, is when, after we think we've achieved something significant, the rug is pulled out from under us. Or we experience the world going backwards, undermining everything we've done, shortly after taking a great step forward. Those steps backwards are often the most clarifying experiences. They tell us that the problem itself wasn't the problem. The real problem lies in the structures of power, most often in politics and in media and in money. So that's where we need to focus most and why FIAT is so important to rally around.

Here are some recent examples of great transformations in civilization, that have been too swiftly undercut:

- In 1964 after a decade of incredible turmoil and centuries of injustice, the American people established the Civil Rights Act. Barack Obama, a black man, was elected President of the United States of America less than 50 years later. It felt like a strong statement of progress. But just eight years after that, the most racist American president in over a century was elected. In the year of his attempted re-election in 2020, over 99 cities in America, largely people of color because of their protests, were teargassed with chemicals that were banned in all war.

- In 1970, we celebrated our first Earth Day. It was a grand celebration. Across the planet we celebrated. Is the Earth in a better place than it was then? No way. There's cleaner air and water in a variety of places, but so many creatures have lost their lives in the last 50 years that didn't need to. And global warming is rapidly enveloping us in a global crisis far greater than anything experienced in human history.

- In 1989 with the fall of the Berlin Wall, it was as if we had suddenly become global citizens, we learned new words, perestroika and glasnost, and thought, "Even Russia is becoming democratic. Democracy has indeed come to the world." There were celebrations across the world for democracy. But in 2016, America elected a president who praised the world's authoritarian leaders as they accumulated greater and greater power, and in 2022 Russia started a war with Ukraine on its border with democratic Europe. Is democracy in a better place now than it was in 1989? I don't think so, and neither do surveys or polls. Dictators have learned quickly to manipulate "the people's vote," as if they were democratic, while instead they accumulated more and more autocratic power.

In each of the above examples, we came to a point where we felt we had won, that the work had been accomplished, and that the world would be a better place permanently for what we had done. But in some perplexing way, years later we found that none of those movements was big enough. We didn't finish the work on any of them. The learning couldn't be clearer. Grassroots movements must be sustained long after apparent victory. If we want a Golden Civilization, after creating the most compelling vision for it, we must build the strongest of foundations, one that will last for thousands of years.

It's time to bring all the causes together and enlist each of our institutions to support them by FIAT. If we can do that, we will have created a world where institutions always have our best interests at heart, where they have become humane. They will be Fiduciary In All Things.

Our freedoms are losing to the growing inequities of money and its accumulation of media power. That is where our real obstacles lie. A quote in August 2017 from former presidential advisor Steve Bannon in *The American Prospect* points at the issue:

> "The longer they talk about identity politics, I got 'em. I want them to talk about racism every day. If the left is focused on race and identity, and we go with economic nationalism, we can crush the Democrats."

The most startling truth here I think can be seen more boldly if we reframe Bannon's statement and make it from the billionaires, media moguls, and corporate czars:

> "If we can keep people focused, outraged, and divided on social issues, they won't see our steady and relentless accumulation of power, won't be able to raise our taxes, limit our monopolies, or touch our political contributions. And with our money, our media power, and our judges and politicians, we will do whatever we like."

We often talk of inequality in terms of wealth and income, but the more insidious inequality, because it's more hidden from us, is the one we don't experience as directly, media power. The less democratic the media is, and the less held to standards of truth, the easier it is to dominate our attention with argumentation or with ignorance, keeping us from seeing the truth that too often the powerful are single-mindedly focused on increasing their power to "crush" their opposition. You can blame the powerful, but our systems are set up to facilitate this.

Over the past 40 years much has changed to give the powerful more power in media, wealth, income, and political influence. In 1983, 50 companies owned 90% of US media. By 2022, five companies owned 90%. Add to that a handful of social media companies and their billionaires, none of them held to journalistic standards of truth, and you can see how our opinions are too often not ours, not freely derived from the truth around us.

It's not just our opinions, but the money that crafts those opinions. In the 2016 presidential election year the richest .01% of the country accounted for 40% of political contributions. That's not the 1% we frequently talk about as having so much wealth compared to the rest of us. That's 1/100th of that 1%, truly the wealthiest of the very wealthy that controlled 40% of political money in the 2016 election. That same percentage of super wealthy accounted for only 15% of political contributions in 1980, just thirty-six years earlier. Inequality can change quickly. Is it any wonder Americans feel unrepresented in their "democracy?" To add insult to injury, "The three richest Americans now own as much as the entire bottom half of the population. The only other country with similarly high levels of wealth concentration is Russia."[12]

---

12 Statistics and quotes from *How America's oligarchy has paved the road to fascism (Why American capitalism is so rotten, Part 7)* Robert Reich, January 2024.

In terms of income, during these same forty years, from 1983 to 2023, the economy as measured by output per worker hour grew by 126%, while worker compensation grew only 27%.[13]

The already powerful have been on a roll since Reagan.

With dramatically rising inequality, media consolidation, and the money of the richest 1/100th of 1% dominating politics, our most significant issue is about our right to have our voices equally heard.

It is time for all media, (and now especially social media) to be held to the standard of the Truth, the Whole Truth, and Nothing but the Truth.

It is not acceptable that people with the greatest power in the world do not share the basic values that are expected of the rest of us. It is unacceptable that those with the most power in the world are not figures of wisdom and compassion, that they do not put people or democracy, truth, or the planet ahead of their own self-interest. Their extreme wealth is repugnant when considered against the poverty of so many. Even more repugnant is that banks choose to lend vast sums to these people and organizations who already abuse their responsibilities to civilization and its people.

What can bring a permanent end to this?

Our work to establish FIAT as the law of the land. Our work to live the Three Domains of Freedom.

---

[13] A 'National and Global Maelstrom' Is Pulling Us Under, by Thomas Edsall; New York Times editorial, January 10, 2024.

Democracy is the greatest freedom we have accomplished in civilization. It facilitates each of our rights and provides the methodologies to increase and improve them. Getting money out of politics and the media is crucial for civilization to thrive. FIAT addresses this issue and many more by stripping all institutions, including those personal incorporations that our richest citizens hide behind, of their freedom to place their self-interest ahead of social obligations, of humanity, truth, Gaia, and democracy.

It is a huge task, but one that is urgent in our time. When placed against the enormous power of wealth and privilege, I take courage from the words of John Lewis and Thomas Paine:

> *Never, ever be afraid to make some noise and get in good trouble, necessary trouble.*
> **— John Lewis**

> *I prefer peace. But if trouble must come, let it come in my time, so that my children can live in peace.*
> **— Thomas Paine**

Our obstacles tell us it's time to act, time to create systemic change that will bring about a sustainable democracy and a civilization of freedom. It is time to make all institutions trustworthy and humane. As we face ever increasing global crises and enormous consolidations of power, there is no time to wait. Rather than overwhelming us, let us use our obstacles to inspire us to action.

We must be vigilant and thorough. Extremes of power and wealth are enabled by loopholes in democracy and freedom. There must be no loopholes. Civilization requires us to stay engaged until the work is completed, until it is sustainable

Domain Three: The Freedom of Civilization

as a domain of freedom. Let's make the vision strong. Let's make it visible to the whole world.

It is our institutions and our "hierarchies of power" that make civilization what it is and that bring its freedoms to all of us. If we are to maintain, build upon, and strengthen these freedoms in a sustainable way, we must be certain that every institution is dedicated to our freedom.

A fiduciary obligation such as FIAT throughout institutional life would quickly establish each of the following:

- Media – It would end dominance by large corporations (profit and non-profit), billionaires, and governments. A free press itself would be Fiduciary in All Things. It would establish fairness, fiduciary and scientific standards. Under all circumstances, humanity could expect media to always speak the Truth, the Whole Truth, and Nothing but the Truth.

- Money would be permanently taken out of politics. It does not support democracy. Banks would not be able to support politicians, nor lend to corporations or billionaires who were not Fiduciaries in All Things.

- Inequality would be dramatically reduced, establishing the principle of freedom for all, by taxing the wealthiest one percent and to the greatest extent the billionaires and centimillionaires and their corporations. A modest guaranteed income for all could be established so that everyone could pursue their life plan with the entrepreneurial fervor imagined in America's Declaration of Independence when it proclaimed each of our rights to life, liberty, and the pursuit of happiness. Ending inequality in this way would enable each person to be the most engaged version of themselves, the person they want to be.

Additionally – A Fiduciary In All Things standard for our institutions:

- Strengthens democracy everywhere.
- Fosters the planet and its species.
- Ends corruption, bigotry, and racism.
- Works in all ways to diminish and eliminate war.
- Ends propaganda, making Truth, the Whole Truth, and Nothing but the Truth the standard for all civilization, for science, for media (including social media), for all corporate, non-profit, or government communication and news.
- Through its commitment to Mother Earth, it facilitates civilizations of freedom everywhere.

At times we have thought of America as the great experiment and at other times we thought it was democracy, but the real experiment is Gaia's and its *Homo sapiens*. If we are to survive or to thrive on Gaia, we must first understand ourselves, and then from that build the institutions that bring out the best in each one of us and in all of us as a species. We must address both inner and outer obstacles, both our fear and despondency, and our systemic support of self-interest and greed over wisdom and compassion. Humans will fail if war is not eliminated, or corruption prevails, or if the planet overheats, if democracy is not established, and if fiduciary responsibility is not sustainably and organically manifested and made the law of the land.

It may mean that at this time each one of us should be VERY ACTIVE politically. At the very least it suggests that we must each live from our Three Domains of Freedom: That we meet moments in a way that brings clarity and authenticity to our every action, that we live the lives we feel called to live, and that we make all of civilization a domain of freedom for everyone. Perhaps only a mass movement can take power away from those who hold onto it. A virtuous movement for freedom and compassion inspires everyone, everywhere, in all corners of the world. It is something to celebrate for all generations.

If the fire inside of us is strong, and we spread our vision across the Earth, nothing can stand in our way.

What if We All Did It?

Civilization would right itself in short order.

There would begin a flourishing of arts and culture, of science and innovation, and of all manner of progress, beyond anything we have ever imagined.

It would mean that civilization is yours, and you would know it. It's not the government's, not the red's or the blue's, not the corporations' or billionaires'. It is ours.

Not only is civilization ours, but it is also who we are, each human being flourishing in their chosen life, in the great community of human beings, each a jewel of civilization.

It would be as if civilization itself had become a virtuous and awakened human being, compassionate and wise, and each of us a change-maker, a leader, of service to others.

So, live your freedom and spread it to all you meet.

Not only can we make this happen, but we must make it happen. And we will.

Civilization will shift, so that the unsustainable problems of humanity that seem so challenging to us will never happen again. Imagine the experience of a sustainable civilization that we can count on for our children, our grandchildren, and all the generations that follow. Imagine what it would mean for all of Earth's creatures.

Domain Three: The Freedom of Civilization

As each of us feels we have a voice and a role, rather than being powerless, society will become far more innovative, expanding the range of our creativity to everything humanly imaginable.

We will lift each other up and never again feel alone.

A civilization of freedom is the greatest possible product of evolution, creating environments where all creatures thrive and flourish.

With the freedom of civilization, we see that the entire species is one species, one people. We no longer divide ourselves from each other by nation or gender or politics or religion or race. More than fellow travelers, we are family. We see clearly that if one person doesn't feel freedom, it impacts all of us. We are more aware and more compassionate toward each of the world's species, each expression of life. We understand ourselves as children of Gaia and as its shepherds. We have more confidence in claiming freedom for all people because it's simply how civilization works. We see so clearly that civilization doesn't work with war or corruption or bigotry, that we can't even imagine that they used to exist, they used to be a norm of our world.

We live in an incredible time, one where a dramatic and global turning for civilization is about to take place. It is a time for transformation, if we are willing to claim it – for ourselves and for all generations to follow. This is what we were meant for.

If we stay programmed, instead, to think we are "one-down" to the rich and powerful, to large institutional forces, we will lose democracy. We will lose the planet.

I have a one generation challenge for each of you. Let us act together. Let us build together now our community of freedom with creativity and kindness and innovation and commitment. If we can do this, in a single generation, within 20 years we will find ourselves in a civilization of freedom, one filled with energy and vitality, with commonality and with hope. And we will have done our work. It's time in the history and evolution of civilization to make this happen.

You're part of the solution. I am too. Let's make a difference.

Civilization is yours.

It's your Third Domain of Freedom.

Conclusion to Civilization as our Third Domain of Freedom

Civilization calls out to you to claim your freedom. Mother Earth calls out to you. The poor and oppressed, the disabled and ignored, the underserved all call out to you to claim your freedom. Your family and friends call out to you to claim your freedom. All creatures call out to you because when you claim your freedom, all of us participate in it. You become the standard for how we might claim our freedom. You become a steward of the whole Earth's freedom and part of the ever-expanding experience of civilization as the Third Domain of Freedom.

Each domain of freedom is connected to all the others. Among them all, civilization is our greatest challenge. It's also our greatest opportunity – to break through our isolation and join at last our whole family, eight billion of us, and billions more if you count all the creatures and life on the planet – to make the world our own.

In spite of our inspiration, with all that needs to be done in civilization and with the great threats to it, and the great powers lined up against our freedoms, it is easy at times to get discouraged, even to spin out in discouragement. When this happens to me, I have learned to quickly shift gears and to go to the one place I can immediately (or very quickly) experience freedom and authenticity – the practice of moments, the First Domain of Freedom. There I find the experience of freedom, of clarity, peaceful and energized.

Looking then at the tasks remaining to deliver the Third Domain of Freedom to all, I remind myself of the timeliness of this work. For the first time in history, we are all connected, as *Homo sapiens*, with immediate access to all the wisdom of humanity and all its practical skills. Ninety percent of us have a smartphone. And for the first time in history, we are aware of how human actions can threaten the whole world. Something must be done by all of us and urgently so. We must throw off the shackles of all our hierarchies of power, by requiring that each and every institution act with humanity toward us all.

I remind myself that by doing this, the challenges for humanity will not end, but a sustainable civilization of freedom will be created that might last for hundreds of thousands of years, giving humanity and perhaps all Earth's creatures the stability and support to live in freedom, and to develop newer and newer environments of freedom for ongoing generations to come. I see both the great value and the necessity of action, action that will bring access to each domain of freedom, to everyone and for all time. And my discouragement is gone.

Civilization is ours.

It is a domain of freedom, our Third Domain of Freedom.

With access to the Three Domains of Freedom, we can live in freedom and bring freedom to others sustainably through all generations.

The Three Domains of Freedom

Final Thoughts

I have come to think of wisdom as the selfless understanding of the present moment and the impermanence that surrounds it. The first domain of the freedom of moments brings us wisdom. And as each moment bursts with energy into our world, it brings us great vitality.

In the first domain, we take comfort and find security regardless of our situation. In the midst of struggle, we find a way to deliver, to communicate, to collaborate, or to find stillness. We let go of our self-absorption, our clinging, our fears and greed, our laziness and doubt. There is no other way to access the present moment. Instead, we see clearly what is and what is required. The complexities of civilization require this clear seeing.

The second domain of freedom grants us permission to thrive, to follow our dreams of freedom and grow into the people we were born to be. What a struggle life becomes if you or I don't feel that we have the freedom to live the life we're meant to live. Civilization struggles as well if we don't deliver the best of ourselves into the world.

The freedom, creativity, and engagement that comes with the second domain gives us confidence to affect change in our communities. Acting together, we self-actualize civilization.

The Three Domains of Freedom give us the freedom to pursue a fulfilled life, to find freedom in any moment, and to change the world.

You have immediate access now to each of the domains:

>Each moment is yours.

>Your life is yours.

>Civilization is yours.

The Three Domains of Freedom answer three of our most profound questions:

1. What is the meaning of life – It is the freedom of moments.
2. What is the meaning of my life – Your life is yours to choose.
3. What is the meaning of the human species and of evolution – Civilization is yours. It is who we are.

As we act on our answers, we become free.

When difficulties arise, it can be helpful to ask yourself, "Where can I find freedom?" Identifying the three domains tells you where freedom is for you right now. Is it to act creatively in civilization, is it to thrive in living your life plan, or is it to pause in the moment itself, feeling your freedom in your step or in your body or in your breath? It can be helpful to hop from domain to domain and just feel yourself flourishing with freedom, wherever you are.

The simplest way to jumpstart your life and embrace the Three Domains of Freedom is to get life planned. It is the centerpiece of freedom because you don't need to form a habit around it as you do with developing a mindfulness practice or engaging with civilization. You get your torch lit and you're off to the races, you're going for it. You have clarity around the direction of your life and what is delivering you into your dreams of freedom and what isn't. Feeling confident that you're on target, your trajectory is strong and exciting and vital. You are delivering your most authentic self into the world.

The second thing? Establish a mindfulness practice. Your inner life is where your authenticity and virtue reside. In each moment, there they are. Mindfulness, with its mastery of the present moment, opens that world up for you in every moment.

Third thing, engage with civilization each day. Take time to recognize how, by participating in civilization and by doing what you already do, you can make civilization a richer domain of freedom for yourself and others, whether at work or in your community or in your family. Take time as well each week to focus on the largest issue you can imagine that would really solve the planet's problems, the species' problems, your country's problems, and then engage. Civilization needs you. It is part of you, part of your thriving.

It is time for each of us to live a life of freedom in each of freedom's domains. It is time for the great flourishing to begin.

Photo by Rachel Kinder

George Kinder is an author and international thought leader.

Known in the financial industry as the Father of Life Planning, George authored three books on money as he revolutionized client-centered financial advice through experiential trainings for thousands of advisors from over 30 countries across six continents.

A mindfulness teacher for thirty-five years and author of the mindfulness primer, *Transforming Suffering into Wisdom*, Kinder has led weekly meditation classes and residential retreats around the world.

Kinder is a published poet and photographer, including his illuminated manuscripts *A Song for Hana* and *Reflections on Spectacle Pond*, a five-volume 'book of hours' for each day and each week of the year, inspiring us to live in the present moment, and to discover it in nature.

His recent books focus on civilization. Understanding civilization as both human evolution and as the evolution of environments of freedom, his passion is to help create a civilization that organically fosters the very best of humanity as it diminishes the very worst.

George and his wife Kathy have two daughters and reside in Massachusetts, while spending several months each year in London and Maui.

Printed in Great Britain
by Amazon